FLOW

How to open the flow of finance for all

PAUL CLEMENTS-HUNT, INGO KUMIC,
MICHAEL MARAIS AND GORDON NOBLE

Print ISBN: 978-1-66784-060-4
eBook ISBN: 978-1-66784-061-1

CONTENTS

PREFACE

The light ripple of initial laughter caught the picture-perfect marquee crowd, and then turned into an almost raucous tsunami of belly laughs. It was one of those truly glorious early summer days in the Kent countryside, the Garden of England, at the end of the year prize giving for a very expensive UK Public School. And the cause of the mirth? The headmaster, wearing an ermine edged cloak representing the tradition of a noble school established in the sixteenth century to serve underprivileged boys, made a seemingly most gentle joke. He had asked the three hundred or so proud parents and staff members seated in the massive canvass structure whether anyone knew what the latest Honourable Guild to be established in the City of London was. Silence. No one knew. "The Honourable Guild of Bankers",[1] he revealed. In a gathered audience containing a significant percentage of bankers, asset managers, traders, insurers, and the lawyers who made fortunes serving the financial sector through the glory years in the run up to the devastating 2007-2008 global financial crash, and its long legacy, the idea of an Honourable Banker was laughable. This moment of mirth was telling. A relaxed community, joined by non-financiers, judging itself as having fallen so far short of honourable and rocking with deep laughter at the thought. Roll back over eighty years to the hard-bitten, industrial city of Liverpool in Northern England, as its communities faced up during the early 1930s to the reality of a catastrophic global depression following on a few years after the financial crash of all crashes, at least until 2007-2008—known to all as The Wall Street Crash. A young mother of four was earning a few extra shillings a week by collecting premiums, door to door, for the Provincial Insurance

Company. As unemployment and abject poverty gripped Liverpool, the woman in her late 20's, walked through her back door one evening and declared, "I am finished with Provincial. They are just crooks. They collect premiums and don't pay out to the families."

The thread running from depression era Liverpool to the green lawns of a wonderful educational establishment some eighty plus years later raises a question. Why does the financial system find it so hard to be honourable? The question itself would raise forceful objections and denunciations from those bankers, investors, insurers, and the often-colourful crowd of characters who make up every nook and so complicated cranny of modern, globalized finance and the multifaceted investment chain underpinning it: "We are nothing but honourable. Look what we achieve for society?" There is truth in that: good finance carried out with vision, creativity and governance can indeed transform societies, industries, and the lives of so many. And yet, as 1929 and 2007-2008 demonstrated, with some many lesser examples in between, so often the finance sector implodes. And the "Honourable Banker" is nowhere to be seen.

Why does it keep going wrong? Geneva mid 2000's pre-crash. A distinguished, old school British Gentleman, a long-time resident of Switzerland, was enjoying a post event cocktail offered by a research company serving the mesmerically wealthy giants of an accelerating hedge fund industry. He had seen it all and made an unlikely fortune doing so. Starting as a twelve-year-old doorboy at the London Stock Exchange in the mid-late 1930s, this quietly smart man had realized early on that the Financial Titans entering the exchange were no smarter than him, and in many cases, far less so. His keen ear picking up banter and tips over the early years as he opened the exchange doors was translated into his own stock trading fortune as he learnt how to play, perhaps manipulate, the markets to his advantage. His telling insight? "It all changed with the Americans and the Big Bang in October 1986", he explained. "Until then The City was a small community, and everyone knew each other. We all knew the bad ones, the rogues, the fraudsters—it was word of mouth. Reputation was everything. We weren't angels but there was honour and it had to be self-policing. It worked to avoid the worst of the excesses." The former LSE doorboy's key point was that the introduction and take-over of electronic trading changed everything: "You used to know everyone heading home on the Tube. It was a club, and you knew who to avoid. With the advent of computers and electronic trading, The City became faceless. Every rogue had a place to hide, and it was mainly behind a computer." Too simple? Perhaps, but there are points to be taken as the electronic trading of early years expanded exponentially as the forces of deregulation, financialization and globalization became the manic mantra of "free markets" as the heady days of the mid-late 1980s, notably in the US and UK, morphed into the boom-bust of the 1990s. The names of countries, institutions and individuals became synonymous with regular financial scandals and crashes from Milken to Mexico and on to Long-Term Capital Management, Russia, the Asian Crash of 1997 and then the dot.com bust and corporate governance road crashes as the Millennium turned. We had to wait a few years for Dick Fuld's Lehman's, the rug enthusiast John Thain, the last Chair and CEO of Merrill Lynch, followed by the 'iconic' fraudster Bernie Madoff, but the thread was always there whether the individual, the institution, or the country.

This book is a book about hope. In the end, the book comes down to a single proposition captured in a single word. Flow. It is the flow of finance to all that ultimately impacts societies and our environment. Flow is the measure by which we understand whether a financial system is serving society. A world where finance does not flow is a world of heightened systemic risks from mass migration of peoples through to unabated climate change. There is a tendency to think that finance is complicated. Books about finance must therefore only be for those that either understand, or want to understand, the intricacies of financial markets. This is not true. Finance at its heart is very simple. Two types of finance – debt and equity – make up the foundations of modern finance. What is complicated is the way that we commonly talk about finance. One of the reasons that the language around finance is so complicated is that there are strong incentives that reinforce finance as a closed system. Money after all is about power. The approach with this book is to tell the story of the power of finance through narratives. The analogy used throughout the book is that finance is like water. Just as water will find a way to flow to its level, so too can finance—if we allow it to. Narratives can also personalize finance and take financial systems beyond numbers to impacts. The book is focused on solutions. Finance can grow businesses that can improve the standard of living across the globe. Finance can support governments to run manageable deficits that ensure the overall stability of society and can address some of the most fundamental challenges facing humanity including climate change. Finance can unlock investments that protect, preserve, and regenerate our environment. An impediment to delivering sustainable development is that finance is not flowing to everywhere that it is needed. The book unpacks why this is the case, and what we can do about it. The changes advocated to open flow of finance to meet the needs of all are practical and achievable without the need for international treaties or changes to domestic legislation. Flow of finance for all is about creating and maintaining the channels that enable finance to reach every corner of the earth and fulfil every need.

INTRODUCTION

The term "cradle of civilization" is attributed to the poet Edmund Spenser, best known for his 1590 epic poem "The Faerie Queene". The term has come to refer to locations in Mesopotamia, Egypt, India, and China where civilizations independently emerged. As soon as humans started to cultivate crops that heralded the start of the Agricultural Revolution, they needed a regular source of water. It is therefore not surprising that "cradles of civilization" are also associated with the first irrigation canals. The core thesis of this book is that just as human intervention created the canals that flowed water to where it was needed, there is a need for intervention to support the establishment of "finance canals" that will open a flow of finance for all. In the 1873 classic text on money, Lombard Street, Walter Bagehot[2] famously wrote, "Thus capital runs as surely and instantly where it is most wanted, and where there is most to be made of it, as water runs to find its level." Bagehot's analogy comparing financial capital with water is still relevant today. Just as water is the key to life, finance is the key to economic life. Without finance businesses cannot grow, jobs are not created, there is no money for climate change adaptation and communities' wither. It has become a cliché to state that there is a need to mobilize trillions of dollars to address systemic challenges such as climate change. One of the core challenges we face in achieving this objective is that in many parts of the world finance has not been flowing at all or has been flowing at such a low rate that it is not meeting the needs of communities. Many words have been dedicated to examining the problems we collectively face. This book does not aim to add to these words. The starting assumption is that you, the reader, have a broad familiarity with the risks of uncontrolled and rampant changes to the world's climate, the current state of inequality and the raft of environmental, social and governance (ESG) issues that threaten economies and the fabric of society. An underlying theme of the book is that sustainability is a systemic issue. There is a tendency in aspects of our lives, whether it be work, or international forums, to structure issues into discrete silos. Whilst there is logic to focus in depth on an issue to solve a particular challenge, creating silos results in blind spots and a failure to see systemic issues that are right before our eyes. Nassim Nicholas Taleb coined the term Black Swan to refer to rare events with an extreme impact that have low predictability. None of the crises we have witnessed recently can be described as Black Swan events. As we shall discuss there were plenty of previous warnings on the dangers of pandemics. Perhaps the greatest surprise with COVID-19 is that a global pandemic had not occurred earlier with SARS and MERS early warnings. Russia's invasion of Ukraine can also not be described as a Black Swan event. There were plenty of warnings that went unheeded. Even if the invasion was analysed solely from a climate change lens (understanding that there were many, many more factors at play), then there is an argument that the re-emergence of resource wars that long characterised empires is not a surprise – and has certainly been actively considered by security analysts. Climate changes impacting Russia include the 1,874,000 km2 Aral Sea Basin which has already been subject to significant warming. The largest freshwater lake in Asia, the 636km Lake Baikal, has already been the subject of tensions with China who faces its own water crises.

The book's core proposition is that by recognising the systemic nature of crises, in response, financial systems need to be structured to flow capital to where it is needed. The question we examine is how can financial systems open flow of finance for all? The term financial system is used quite deliberately. This is not a book about the finance sector. Financial systems consist of a broader range of participants than the finance sector, which represent those financial institutions that serve the system. Financial systems include governments, regulators, banks, insurers, investors as well as households and business. An underlying theme of the book is that many participants do not appreciate that they are part of a financial system, and do not participate in shaping it. Examples include municipal authorities that have the power to not only borrow from financial markets but have the power to create financial markets themselves. The tendency to think of finance through the lens of the finance sector, rather than as a financial system, results in a bias where questions on solutions to sustainability challenges are seen through the prism of financial products. Financial products do have a fundamental role to play in flowing finance to all, however, they are not the only lever that can be pulled to achieve outcomes. The book argues that there is a need to establish mechanisms that encourage innovation. Financial systems need to become open systems that consider and facilitate different ways of doing things. An example of an open system is the early development of information technology, with owners of IBM computers in the 1950's collaborating with each other to develop tools to improve the use of their computers. The open-source software movement can be credited with a score of innovations that have led to many of the applications that we take for granted today. An area where financial systems have been embracing the principles of the open-source software movement is responsible investment. Responsible investment has grown from a niche of the financial system to become mainstream within fifteen years. Language such as environmental, social and governance (ESG), which was first developed by responsible investors to succinctly communicate the need to consider all factors that influence the long-term value of an investment, not just the financial factors contained in financial statements, provides a common language around which financial system participants can debate issues. Through the leadership of institutions such as the United Nations Environment Program Finance Initiative (UNEPFI), thousands of individuals within financial institutions have been able to overcome the closed systems of their organizations and exchange ideas globally. One of the key challenges today is how the sustainable finance community can operate as an open system as concepts such as ESG become mainstream.

A range of critical opportunities to build sustainable financial markets, which can deliver for all 7.8 billion on the planet climbing to 9-10 billion by the Century's close, are considered. To deliver the UN Sustainable Development Goals (SDGs),[3] financial systems need to focus on the creation of local markets that deliver development outcomes at real scale. The book examines the ways that financial system participants, including governments and regulators, impede the flow of finance to sustainable development. The fundamental role of a financial system is to allocate capital. Scanning the horizon of the global financial system it is evident that there are major gaps where, due to factors including investor behaviour and regulatory practices, finance is simply not flowing. For instance, through an understanding of why institutional investors herd into large pools of what can be called 'timid capital',[4] the strengths of the system can be used to design interventions that will flow capital to where it is needed. As financial systems grapple with the allocation of capital to areas including provision of infrastructure services, repair of natural systems, addressing inequality and investing in communities in developing countries and frontier economies, there is a need to understand how financial markets are created. To do that there is a need to go back into history. Historically, markets were always local. A key insight from the historic development of stock exchanges is that the key invention that created the first stock exchange was the establishment of a mechanism to transfer an asset from one person to another. It was not, as we may commonly think, to price an asset. This insight has implications in the development of new markets in areas including natural capital and impact investment. The establishment of market architecture that facilitates trading is critical to the scaling of new innovations in sustainable finance. Governments have always played a critical role in establishing and governing markets and have a key role to play in creating new financial markets that open finance for all.

The book presents a range of ideas on how to open flow of finance across a broad range of communities including refugees, remote and rural communities that lack access to infrastructure, and less developed countries. The disruption of infrastructure through technology is offering the opportunity to deliver core infrastructure services such as delivery of energy and water to all people, no matter where they live. The book outlines an ambition for Universal Infrastructure Coverage (UIC) that is possible today through three simple propositions: Firstly, recognize that the emergence of distributed infrastructure is a game changer that creates the possibility of universal infrastructure coverage. Secondly, establish infrastructure as a business that is co-owned by governments and institutional investors and that is listed on local stock exchanges. Thirdly, support the management of infrastructure businesses through the development and implementation of stewardship principles.

Addressing the poverty premium—the extra cost that households on low incomes incur when purchasing the same essential goods and services as households on higher incomes—requires addressing access to finance. To outline the opportunity for innovation we outline the concept of a Refugee Income Contingent Loan Scheme to provide access to finance to the 60 million refugees and internally displaced people across the globe. A Sustainable Finance for Refugees Initiative (SFRI) is proposed as a means through which separate UN bodies can work together. We use the term Financial System Impact Regulation to describe how nudges to financial regulatory systems can facilitate a flow of finance for all. For regulators to support Financial System Impact Regulation there needs to be coordination, which can occur through the leadership of the G20 Sustainable Finance Working Group.

Communities are at the frontline of the impacts of climate change and inequality. In simple terms the SDGs, including addressing climate change, cannot be met unless there is a focus on communities. When society is not in balance, the results can be conflict and volatility that ultimately harm us all—communities, financial system participants, stakeholders, and governments. When communities are in balance, they can respond to challenges—whether it be changing climate, supporting health for all, or creating economic opportunities. Community infrastructure has become the forgotten infrastructure but is critical for local community development.

Mechanisms such as securitization can be applied to open blended municipal bond markets with Community Partnership Agreements providing the mechanism to bring diverse stakeholders together.

Dialogue across financial systems and with a variety of stakeholders including NGOs, governments and regulators requires a new form of institutional architecture. Creating a broad financial system dialogue has the potential to address one of the unstated impediments to financing sustainable development, which is that the finance sector tends to operate as a closed system within a financial system. The need for privacy of information is one reason why financial services organizations operate as a closed system. A closed system is however itself a major impediment to innovation. A critical challenge is how we create opportunities outside of the finance sector. Forging collaborative coalitions with all stakeholders including governments, regulators, business, civil society, and financial system participants is critical to the flow of finance for all. The elements that must come together to drive transformation are the establishment of platforms for collaboration amongst diverse groups and preparedness to support innovations to address system impediments. Cross-Sector Implementation Facilities (CSIF) are proposed as a mechanism to catalyse blended capital into place-based impact through the scaling of fit-for-purpose enterprise structures. A foundation of successful CSIF's is their ability to engage with financial markets and be visible within the financial system. CSIF are distinct from other delivery forms and structures due to their use of blended finance approaches involving 'patient capital' and the pursuit of sustainable change management.

Other ideas in the book are focused on human capital and biodiversity. A Human Capital Strategic Engagement Model is proposed as a mechanism to improve long term performance of a company's most important asset—its people. The model is based around risk management practices that are commonly used in the corporate sector and consists of a simple traffic light system to identify risk. The intention of the Human Capital Strategic Engagement Model is to link into market indicators of human capital performance. Financing biodiversity at scale is proposed through

Blended Biodiversity Bonds as part of a broader Biodiversity Bond Market. The nature of biodiversity is that each species, and each ecosystem is unique. Understanding the unique needs of each species and each ecosystem is critically important to open a flow of finance for biodiversity. A Biodiversity Bond Market would consist of blended biodiversity bonds with partnerships at their core. There is a logic that water utilities take on a leadership role in developing what has the potential to become a significant market. There is an opportunity for water utilities to collaborate globally to support the establishment of a Biodiversity Bond Initiative, which would scale the financing of biodiversity.

What is the cost of inaction? With just 10 percent of the world's stock exchanges containing 90 percent of market capitalization, if financial system participants persist with models that result in the herding of financial capital, then the result will be an increase in system risk. Using our water analogy, if the world had one giant dam that held 90 percent of the world's fresh water supply, what would the risks be to humanity? Not only would most of the world's population be deprived of water, but the dam itself would be a source of risk if it was to burst. But this is the situation that currently faces us. The accumulation of capital into a few stock exchanges creates system risk. If communities are starved of capital, there is a danger that the two-tier world of "haves and have nots" will create ongoing system risks. Without change "timid capital" will miss out on the scale, vibrancy and potential of frontier and emerging market investments. Such investments will include the SME base in non-OECD countries and the last mile entrepreneurs starting to disrupt traditional value and supply chains by taking advantage of the blossoming convergence of digital, pay-as-you go (PayGo), fintech, machine learning (ML), artificial intelligence (AI), e-mobility/drone technology, and the "Internet of things (IoT)".

In an era of financial globalization, the emergence of massive pools of capital controlled by a limited number of markets means many billions of people will be left behind unless finance is re-imagined. But can finance be re-imagined? The fundamental change that is needed is culture change.

Culture change within a financial system? Absolutely. Culture change is required along the entire finance chain from the ultimate beneficiaries of pension funds and insurance reserves, that invest in corporations whose innovation and risk-taking drive growth, to the banks that lend to households and small businesses that drive local economies.

How can the ideas in this book be taken forward? This is the fundamental challenge. Governments and regulators need to be prepared to drive change. The raft of proposals that are outlined do not require international treaties, lengthy negotiations, legislation, or government inquiries. They can be implemented progressively today if there is commitment to change.

In the end, delivering change is not about the ideas but about the willingness to collaborate, the need to build trust and at core the need for empathy. There is hope for the future. As Ralph Waldo Emerson said, "the creation of a thousand forests is in one acorn."

THE FOUNDATIONS OF FLOW

To explore the question on how to flow finance for all, we need a starting point. We need to understand where we have come from, and the progress that has so far been achieved. Gaziantep may seem an unlikely place to reflect on the flow of finance for all. Located in Turkey's Anatolia region, the city is famous for its mosaics and its baklava. It is also just 97 kilometres north of Aleppo in Syria. By 2015, 2 million refugees had passed through the city. In one 24-hour period alone, 200,000 refugees arrived. The city itself successfully hosted 560,000 refugees.[5] The city's success at integrating refugees into its economy and society was the reason that it was chosen in November 2019 by the United Nations Development Program (UNDP) to host the International Forum on Local Solutions to Migration and Displacement.[6] Mayors from 13 countries and 4 continents met with stakeholders from UN agencies, governments, municipalities, cities, international and local NGOs, the private sector and civil society, and adopted the Gaziantep Declaration, highlighting a pathway for refugees from emergency to resilience and development that includes a focus on scaling job creation and partnerships with the private sector at the local level. Through participation at the Forum,[7] we were able to reflect on the ways in which financial systems could innovate to open access to finance for the 79.5 million people that today have been forcibly displaced from their homes.[8] The opportunity to create new innovations to unlock finance for refugees is discussed later in the book. The history of the city itself provided an opportunity to reflect on the broader challenge of financing sustainable development. Dating back to 3,500 BC, Gaziantep is one of the oldest cities in the world. The city was critical to the Persian Royal Road and the Silk Road trade routes that fundamentally shaped civilization. When it comes to thinking about the history of the Silk Road, the mental image that arises is of donkeys and horses burdened with cargoes travelling long distances along dusty tracks. The stone pillars of Gaziantep's caravanserai vividly tell the story that the Silk Road was far more deeply embedded into society. Caravanserais on the Persian Royal Road and Silk Road were not just roadside inns where travellers could rest. They were significant pieces of infrastructure that were built and maintained to facilitate trade. In some parts of the Muslim world, caravanserais also provided revenues that were used to fund charitable or religious functions or buildings. These revenues and functions were managed through a protected agreement which gave certain buildings and revenues the status of a waqf[9], Arabic for endowment. A modern translation is that caravanserais operated as mutual structures where the owners were the community. From a financial system perspective, the caravanserais on the Persian Royal Road and Silk Road can also be seen as a form of market infrastructure. We will examine the importance of market structures to open a flow of finance for all later in the book. Whilst visitors to Gaziantep are today attracted to the refurbished caravanserai, which now host international functions, another of the city's ancient treasures is hidden from view. The city sits on the Gaziantep Plateau. The region has hot summers and does not have the mighty rivers upon which it could build a civilization as the Mesopotamian empires did with their location next to Tigris and Euphrates and the Egyptians did with the Nile. The geological structure of the Gaziantep Region also does not allow lakes to be formed as water seeps into the limestone ground. This led the early pioneers to go underground to carve tunnels to bring and distribute water across the city. Gaziantep has an extensive system of water tunnels known as livas and water structures known as kastels that have been recognized for their cultural significance by UNESCO. Kastels are the point where the livas are made publicly available and consist of pools, wells, sitting places, mosques, water closets and places for bathing that can be considered as form of municipal social service.[10] Gaziantep's livas and kastels are just one example of the way civilizations have directed the flow of water to where it is needed. The oldest known canals were built in Mesopotamia circa 4000 BCE. The Egyptians' ancient Canal of the Pharaohs was "rediscovered" by Napoleon in 1799. Rome's first aqueduct was built in 312 BCE, and the Industrial Revolution was supported by the establishment of the Bridgewater Canal in 1761 between Worsley and Manchester, which resulted in the price of coal halving and "Canal Mania" spreading across Britain. In our modern economy, the mega Suez and Panama canals have played a key role in opening global trade in the twentieth century.

When Napoleon invaded Egypt in 1798, he was told that the Red Sea was thirty feet higher than the Mediterranean. Digging a canal, he was told, would result in the Red Sea pouring into Mediterranean resulting in catastrophe. The argument although wrong repeated Darius, King of Persia's belief in 500 BC that at the time prevented the Persians from digging a canal. The ancients knew that flow is subject to simple physical mechanics. The flow of finance is similarly based on fundamentals. The foundations of finance at its heart are actually very simple. Two products, debt and equity are the foundations of how a financial system flows finance to all. Financial markets are the mechanism through which debt and equity are transacted. As anthropologist David Graeber argues,[11] debt preceded money in ancient societies and is linked to bondage and slavery. The banking system that we know today grew out of institutions such as the Republic of Genoa's Bank of Saint George, which was founded in 1407 to consolidate public debt and finance the medieval kingdoms as well as to fund the exploits of Christopher Columbus. The concept of debt itself is simple. In return for borrowing money, interest is paid to the lender. The scale of borrowing depends on the capacity of the individual or entity. In our modern society, an individual may borrow money to buy a house or a car while a nation may borrow money to finance its spending. According to the International Monetary Fund (IMF), prior to the COVID-19 pandemic, public and private debt reached 225 percent of GDP.[12] The Institute of International Finance estimates that the global level of debt to GDP rose in Q1 2021 was 289 trillion dollars or 360 percent of global GDP.[13]

Equity is the share of ownership of an asset. Historically, assets were physical, but the concept of the corporation gave rise to the ability to own a share of a company. The value of an asset might be thought of as an indicator of optimism. In war time, for instance, the most precious assets can become food, water, and gold. In our modern society, individuals have equity in the assets they own such as houses and cars. There are two principal types of equity investments. Listed equity investments are held on publicly traded stock exchanges while unlisted equity investments are held privately. The common way to value a business is by listing it on a local stock exchange. According to the World Federation of Exchanges (WFE), the global capitalization of ninety-eight stock exchanges as of November 2020 amounted to USD 109.21 trillion.[14] The key difference between debt and equity is that there is no guarantee on the level of return for equity whereas the rate of return for debt is generally capped. The mechanism that enables the flow of debt and equity is the market. Whether buying and selling of fruit and vegetables or trading of financial securities, markets are subject to the principles of supply and demand. In theoretical economic models, participants in a market have access to perfect information. Price is then the mechanism through which supply and demand reach equilibrium. Financial markets are however different from a fruit and vegetable market where an individual may physically walk away with an apple after paying for it. The ownership of a large corporation requires mechanisms to acknowledge property rights. Enabling an individual to transfer ownership to another individual is core the operation of financial markets. For assets that involve a right to an ongoing or future benefit, there is a need for some form of paperwork to demonstrate that ownership has transferred. In the case of physical goods such as a car, an individual registers a transfer of ownership with the relevant transport authority. From a purely theoretical perspective, it is possible to register the ownership of different kinds of assets including a train ticket to a gym membership. In practical terms, registration of assets is focused on assets with high values such as land.

The development of markets to facilitate the flow of goods has been a foundation of economies and societies. In the United Kingdom, the *Domesday Book*, compiled in 1086, recorded sixty market towns. Historically, it was governments that directed the formation of market towns. The gathering of a market around a town square was not only convenient for traders but enabled local lords to control the activities of the market. Medieval European market towns also provided local lords with a valuable source of income. Stall holders were required to pay "stallage" and tolls were levied on all goods brought into town with officials appointed to inspect weights and measures with powers to issue fines. Language we still use today, such as the word forestall, which referred to a stall holder selling before the market, arose out of the development of market towns.[15] Whilst the convening and control of place was critical to the establishment of market towns, the origins of the world's first modern stock exchange in 1602, brilliantly captured by Lodewijk Petram,[16] reveals that the transfer of ownership of a share, which became a foundation of modern stock exchanges, happened by accident, not design. Petram outlines the history of the Dutch East India Company (Verenigde Oost-Indische Compagnie, VOC) and its first "initial public offering" in August 1602. The core purpose of the Dutch East India Company was to gather sufficient finance to commission a flotilla to travel to the Dutch East Indies (Indonesia) to bring back cargoes of coffee, tea, cacao, tobacco, rubber, sugar, and opium. Normally, flotillas operated for three to four years with the proceeds from cargoes sold and profits distributed to private investors. The challenge that the founders of the Dutch East India Company needed to address as they sought to attract investors through their invitation to "All the residents of these lands" to "buy shares in this Company," was the time length of the company's charter. By proposing that a private investor's money would be locked up for twenty-one years, the Dutch East India Company needed to establish a process where an investor's share of the enterprise could be traded to another person. The company's capital subscription register stated that "Conveyance or transfer [of shares] may be done through the bookkeeper of this chamber."[17] In practical terms the buyer and the seller of a share, or their authorized representatives, "had to appear together before the company bookkeeper, and two directors had to approve the transfer before it became official. The bookkeeper kept a large ledger in which every shareholder had an account. If a shareholder sold a share, his or her account was debited by the amount concerned. And if he or she bought a share, the account was credited".[18] The importance of the Dutch East India Company's charter was to outline clear rules to transfer the ownership of shares. In modern terms, the Company's bookkeeper provided the role of a clearinghouse. Whilst authorities in Amsterdam tried to regulate where the trading of shares would take place, the reality was that share trading occurred across the city from morning to night with the trade then confirmed through an official transfer of ownership.[19] The impact of what at the time seemed like an innocuous innovation was that the Dutch East Indies Company was able to raise ten times the capital of the British East Indies Company, which in turn resulted in huge profits with dividends of up to 3,600 percent at a time when the British East India company was struggling to deliver a dividend at all.[20] Trading of Dutch East India Company shares illustrates that the process to transfer an asset from one person to the next was the key to unlocking financial markets. This is a critical point that is worth repeating. The key invention that led to the development of modern financial markets was the establishment of a governance mechanism to transfer an asset from one person to another. It was not, as we commonly think, to price an asset. In fact, it was almost a hundred years later in 1698 when the London Stock Exchange was established in Jonathan's Coffee House where John Castaing established the practice of posting a list of stock and commodity prices called, "The Course of the Exchange and other things".[21], An efficient financial market however requires more than trading of assets. Research by Goshen and Ovsky[22] has argued that information plays a critical role in establishing an efficient market. Three components of market information are identified. Information production involves searching for currently unknown information that affects prices. Accuracy verification involves actions necessary to confirm the reliability of the information source and the credibility of the information. Pricing information requires analysing the information to determine its value, and then trading based on discrepancies between price and value. Goshen and Ovsky argue that mandatory disclosure is essential to the efficient functioning of a stock market. "Absent mandatory disclosure duties, information traders would engage in duplicative efforts to uncover non-public information. The cost of these efforts would be extremely high because information traders, as outsiders, lack access to the management of the firm. Disclosure duties pass these costs to the individual firm".[23] Even in medieval market towns brokers existed to provide matchmaking between buyers and sellers. Research on the regulation of medieval market towns[24] reveals that brokers would pay an annual fee to the city council for the lease of their business. Brokers played a role as intermediaries across a wide range of goods including salt, wine, horses, spices, and construction materials. The responsibility of brokers varied but included informing the buyer of the quality of the goods being purchased. Brokers were not entitled to engage in trade themselves. Penalties for breaching council regulations included fines, loss of rights to broker and imprisonment. An added dimension to the efficient functioning of a financial market is trust. United States criminologist Dr. Donald Cressey[25] examined the rationale behind establishing and enforcing rules for market integrity goes back to 1953. Cressey interviewed one hundred thirty-three inmates in three penitentiaries who had misused a position of financial trust. His resulting "fraud triangle", which has become the core of financial markets, consisted of three components that work together to contribute to increasing the risk of fraud: (1) opportunity, (2) incentive, and (3) rationalization. To counter the risk of fraud, financial regulators have focused on the importance of market integrity. Janet Austin[26] has examined the importance of market integrity for securities regulation and argues that it requires the elimination of market abuse activities, that is, behaviours whereby one person takes advantage of their position to gain an unmerited advantage over another. This includes insider trading, market manipulation and front running. Austin identifies factors critical to market integrity as including non-discriminatory access to the market for all those wishing to participate, transparent and accurate information about the price of securities available to all participants at the same time and accurate information about issuers of securities available to all participants at the same time.

For finance to flow for all there is a need to establish new markets as well as reform existing ones. There are many areas of need where efficient markets do not exist, such as financing biodiversity investments that will be discussed later in the book. When it comes to considering the development of new markets it is important to understand that the foundation of any market is the concept of scarcity. Scarcity refers to the gap between limited (scarce) resources and theoretically limitless wants. Scarcity can occur through limited resources. Government regulation is one way in which an asset can be given scarcity, which in turn gives it value. An example is the extraction of natural resources. The imposition of a requirement by government that to catch fish or harvest trees there is a need to pay a commercial license fee, introduces scarcity into what otherwise would be a free good. A commercial fishing license or forestry license has transfer value because government has placed a limit on the ability to otherwise extract what was (wrongly) regarded as a "free" resource. Recent developments in blockchain technology have illustrated that scarcity can be artificially created through a non-fungible token (NFT). NFT is a digital file whose unique identity and ownership are verified on a blockchain that is not mutually interchangeable.

Having established the foundations upon which financial markets are based we shall now examine in detail the way in which modern financial markets operate. Unlike the flow of water upon which civilization has been based, finance is not flowing to where society needs. To open a flow of finance for all there is a need to understand how it is that the world's accumulated capital flows to large financial markets, why it stays trapped there, and most importantly what is needed to open a flow of finance to all.

CAPTURING FLOW

Around 7,000 years ago Faiyum in Egypt became one of the world's first agricultural regions. Under the rule of Amenemhet I, 4,000 years ago the Egyptians began trapping the annual flood of the Nile River through the natural Lake Faiyum. Egyptian farmers would build mud-brick reservoirs to trap flood waters on their land, using irrigation channels to distribute water to where it was needed. The development of ancient cities not only required the distribution of water to where it was needed through channels, but also required the water to be trapped and accumulated in the first place.

Stock exchanges are both the reservoirs and canals of financial systems. Capital flows into stock exchanges, which then funds businesses. The amount of capital that flows into a stock exchange can be seen as a measure of its potential to finance sustainable development. According to the World Federation of Exchanges (WFE), there are ninety-eight stock exchanges that as of November 2020 held assets that were valued at USD 109.21 trillion.[27] The largest stock exchange in the world, the New York Stock Exchange, had an equity market capitalization over USD 25 trillion in April 2020. The combined market capitalization of NYSE, NASDAQ, Hong Kong, Shanghai, Tokyo Stock Exchange, Euronext, Shenzen, London Stock Exchange, and the Toronto Stock Exchange is around USD 80 trillion. To translate that, just 10 percent of the world's stock exchanges contain 90 percent of total market capitalization. Modern financial markets are in fact working in ways to trap the flow as the Egyptians once did to capture the waters of the Nile. The problem is the flow of finance is accumulating into a small number of exchanges without a mechanism to ensure that the benefits of flow are distributed evenly. Why is financial capital being trapped in a small number of financial markets? And perhaps more importantly, is this a good thing for society?

To answer this question, we need to go back to understand a major shift in capital that started to become evident in the 1970's. In 1976, renowned management consultant Peter Drucker wrote *The Pension Fund Revolution* in which he argued that the growth of pension funds would ultimately impact on the allocation of capital and management practices. The first chapter of the book, "The Revolution No One Noticed", laid out how the decision by General Motors (GM) to introduce a pension for its workers in April 1950 subsequently led to an explosion in the establishment of new pension plans with eight thousand established in a single year. Drucker saw that the growth of pension funds would be a permanent change in capital. At the time, he was concerned that pension funds trustees did not have the skills to be entrepreneurs and argued that the 'person who is investing in what already exists, is in effect trying to minimize risk'. Recognizing the economic problems that existed at the time in the US economy, he believed that the rise of pension fund investing was a unique opportunity to restore the legitimacy of management arguing that 'pension fund management requires and deserves an independent institution, divorced from commercial banking, investment banking or any other banking business'.[28] Drucker believed that pension funds needed to be long term investors, stating that whilst for most people 'maximizing shareholder value' means a higher share price within six months or a year, such short-term capital gains are the wrong objective for both the enterprise and its dominant shareholders.[29] In 1995, Drucker re-published *The Pension Fund Revolution* adding an epilogue on the governance of corporations in which he warned that 'pension funds cannot be managers as were so many nineteenth century owners'. Drucker argued that there is a need for new institutional structures that support pension funds to keep management accountable. He stated, "A business, even a small one needs strong, autonomous management with the authority, continuity and competence to build and run the organization". Pension funds, as America's new owners, Drucker argued would increasingly have to make sure that a company has the management it needs with accountability institutionally anchored.[30] Drucker's solution to build management accountability was to propose a business audit that would be conducted by an independent professional agency every three years and this agency would sit alongside the financial audit. It would be based on pre-determined standards and go through a systematic evaluation of business performance; starting with mission and strategy, through marketing, innovation, productivity, people development, community relations, all the way to profitability.[31] Drucker's conclusion that the rise of pension fund investment would impact on the real economy proved to be accurate. But instead of moving towards an independent business audit as he advocated, investors instead turned to the work of American economist Harry Markowitz. Markowitz's 1952 essay on Modern Portfolio Theory (MPT) introduced the concepts of the risk return trade-off, correlations in returns of different assets, portfolio selection and investment optimization. Building an investment portfolio was about choosing the level of risk that the investor is prepared to accept. MPT's Efficient Frontier provides a theoretical framework where an investor can select the level of risk they are prepared to accept. By mixing 'risk free assets' with a portfolio of securities on the Efficient Frontier, an investor is theoretically able to identify the most risk efficient portfolio. One of the core tenets of MPT is the concept of diversification in investing. By selecting a collection of assets, an investor is theoretically able to select different types of assets whose values change at different times. The concept of 'correlation' provides a mechanism to measure the extent to which asset values move together. The best example of this is share prices and bond prices that will behave in different ways according to the economic cycle. By determining an asset allocation based on the expected behaviour of different assets, an investor is theoretically able to build a portfolio that matched their risk and return objectives. Whilst MPT is good in theory, the problem is that institutional investors took it literally. MPT became the dominant investment paradigm, not only in the US but globally. The beauty of MPT was that it allowed, and still allows, investors to build large investment portfolios with very few resources. In contrast, Drucker's proposal for a business audit focused on the innovation of the company would have required changes to policy settings, which would not have been easy to achieve—particularly when there was at that stage no agreement that the existing practices needed changing. For the trustees of publicly owned pension funds serving teachers, police, emergency services and health workers, the low cost of MPT was particularly attractive. It meant that pension funds were able to accumulate significant assets at very low cost. Over recent years the application of MPT has evolved with the trend to drive costs down by using an approach known as passive investing. The best example of passive investing is the Norwegian Government Pension Fund Global (GPFG), more commonly known as the Norwegian oil fund, which manages over USD 1.25 trillion of assets with a management cost of just over 5 basis points.[32] The fund invests in nine thousand companies with the reality that the fund's trustees know very little about each company it invests in. As at March 2020, US stocks held in passive portfolios accounted for about 14 percent of the domestic equity market, up from less than 4 percent in 2005. According to the UN-supported Principles for Responsible Investment, it is believed that there is now a greater volume of assets following passive strategies than there is in active investment funds.[33] Overall it is estimated that the global passive investment industry manages USD 15 trillion in assets.[34] The growth of passive investment as an investment strategy is one of the reasons why large institutional investors such as pension funds and sovereign wealth funds flow capital into the financial markets that have the deepest pools of capital. This is not the only mutually reinforcing aspect of the financial system that leads to a constant flow of finance to the largest financial markets in the world. Other mutually reinforcing policies that support the accumulation of assets in a small number of very large pools include the establishment of policies by pension fund trustees which are supported by financial system regulators to only invest in liquid investments, or to only invest in highly rated bonds. Whilst mutually reinforcing practices may seem prudent from the perspective of an individual pension fund, because pension funds and sovereign wealth funds around the world employ the same strategies, they result in the magnification of systemic risks. MPT and its associated practices results in a perverse impact on the flow of finance. Examples include sovereign wealth funds that hold the precious assets of a developing country, which will flow those assets to financial markets that do not invest in their country. The combination of modern portfolio theory, requirements for market liquidity for investment, rating of bonds and passive investment strategies have the impact of trapping the flow of capital.

FLOW AND TRANSITIONS

Gaziantep's ancient system of livas and kastels are the means through which water flows through the city. Livas are the water tunnels carved into the limestone earth whilst kastels are the exit points for the water that enable public use. United Nations Educational, Scientific and Cultural Organization (UNESCO) describes Gaziantep's kastel in the following way, "Kastels are quite comprehensively planned structures that include spatial arrangements for many different functions, serving as pools, wells, sitting places, small mosques, water closets and places for bathing. With these functions, kastels, together with the water-related service areas, has become an important meeting place in the daily social life of the city where people come together, spend time, do their work, and perform their religious worship. They were also used to cool off during hot summer days. With the possibilities provided by these structures, they have brought along an important municipal social service". Another means by which ancient Egyptian and Mesopotamian societies distributed water to the last mile was through the shaduf, a simple crane-like tool that enables water to be scooped up from a canal or well and spread across fields to irrigate crops. Once ancient civilizations conquered the flow of water for agricultural and urban populations, attention turned to other ways to harness the power of water. In his dedication to the emperor Augustus Roman engineer Vitruvius was the first to record the use of a waterwheel in his *Ten Books on Architecture*. It wasn't until the tenth century that the use of waterwheels took off in Europe. The *Domesday Book* in 1086 lists 5,624 water mills used for grounding wheat. A century before there were believed to have only been 100 mills.[35] There are several arguments as to why the number of waterwheels increased, including progress in land reclamation and increased cultivation of grain. The history of civilization is that water flowed to everywhere it was needed. Everyone had access to water in ancient cities. Every citizen had the right to access a flow of water because it was essential to the ability to live. The flow of finance needs to be seen in the same way. If a financial system is designed in a way that takes finance to the people, then through simple tools equivalent to the ancient shaduf finance can flow to all. Flow of finance to all has however become blocked or flows at a trickle that is not sufficient to meet the needs of communities. The challenge with the accumulation of capital in the world's largest financial markets is that it distorts financial systems towards larger scale investments. There is no doubt that large scale investments have been critical to social and economic development over the centuries. But to be truly transformative they need to be accompanied by investments at every level of society. An example is the transition from wooden sailing ships to iron hulled ships, which took place from 1780 to 1900.[36] Frank W. Geels charts the evolution of steam ships from the first experiments occurring in the late eighteenth and early nineteenth century in Britain, France, and America, which took place in inland waterways that then led to market innovations including the first steamboat service in America established on the Hudson River in 1807. According to Geels, the evolution of shipping included the development of networks of specialized middlemen facilitating the circulation of information, including journals of prices (1795), commercial newspapers (c. 1815), mercantile libraries (1820), trade journals (1831), ship-to-shore semaphore systems (1830s), agencies for advertising (1841), and credit report books distributed by subscription (1844). The British government supported the development of steamships from 1838 when it subsidized mail on specific trade routes supporting a global network of British intercontinental steam companies. Mail subsidies, it has been argued, supported new technical trajectories to emerge including screw propulsion, iron hulls, and more efficient steam engines. As iron-hulled steam ships gained ascendancy, they firstly took on the profitable Atlantic routes. Critically, one of the long-term impacts of the transition from sail to steam was the new focus on speed, which enabled further innovations ultimately resulting in a shift of cargo from commodities to migrants. For countries such as Australia this was a turning point that opened-up mass migration. The key point here is that the transformation of shipping, which ultimately changed societies by opening migration, could not have happened only through large scale investments in iron-hulled ships but required the development of a supporting ecosystem of businesses. If flow of finance is constrained, then ultimately the rate of innovation is slowed. Flow of finance leads to the potential for new innovations that would not have been thought possible. There have been many examples in the past demonstrating how a flow of finance has led to a spark that has created an economic transition. In addition to the transition from sailing ships to iron-hulled steam ships, the development of the automobile and in our generation the rise of computers and information technology all resulted in changes that were impossible to predict at the time. Each of these economic transitions went through stages where the provision of new finance to the last mile was key to unlocking the next stage of innovation.

Efforts to develop the automobile began with Nicholas Joseph Cugnot (1755), William Murdock (1780), Richard Trevithick (1801) but it can be argued that it was with the world's first auto race in Paris in July 1894 that the era of the automobile began. The tipping point for car manufacturing was Ford's Model T, which took the automobile from a luxury good to a mass consumer good. In 1909, Ford manufactured 10,666 Model T Fords. By 1913, Ford was manufacturing 170,211 cars.[37] The development of the automobile at the turn of the twentieth century required many innovations including in mining, engine, and tire development. The development of low-cost cars also supported the development of newspapers with advertising and editorials key to building consumer awareness and confidence. In addition to inadvertently supporting the newspaper industry, the development of automobiles stimulated investment in associated infrastructure such as roads and petrol stations. In countries like Australia, the first gas stations were hotels. It was not until 1936 that a network of petrol stations was developed through the incorporation of the Australian Motorists Petrol Company (AMPOL). Ultimately, the development of the automobile had significant impacts on urban development, enabling suburbs to sprawl and enabling the growth of cities.

From the development of punch card machines in 1890, to the early prototype computer Harvard Mark 1 in 1944 to the development of Microsoft's Windows in 1983, Walter Isaacson tracks the evolution of the digital revolution. Isaacson demonstrates how innovations led to new innovations. While government contracts and universities influenced the development of information technology, Linus Torvald's decision to release his open-source operating system Linux to a peer-to-peer volunteer collaboration network illustrates the many hands that are required to drive a transition. Today we are still amid the digital revolution. Already we have seen the impact of the growth of businesses such as Amazon, Apple, Google, and Microsoft on traditional industries including newspapers, photography, and department stores. Where the digital revolution ends will only be known over the coming decades. What the digital revolution is reaffirming is that transitions inevitably result in dislocation. In the case of the transition from wooden-hulled vessels to iron, the ship building city of Bristol ultimately lost competitiveness because the Avon River was unable to support larger iron-hulled vessels. The rise of the automobile resulted in the development of industrial cities such as Detroit while evolutions in information technology decimated traditional industries and opened-up new industries. Economic transitions can result in social pain as was demonstrated with the transition of the textile industry in the nineteenth century, which led to the emergence of the Luddites—a secret oath-based organization group that destroyed textile machinery as a form of protest that in turn led to the development of trade unions. The tendency of innovation to disrupt economies and societies means that governments have an important role to play in supporting communities through transitions.

The nature of transitions is that one innovation can lead to subsequent innovations. An example is the story of the ice industry. As Robert Gordon Jr. points out in his book, *The Rise and Fall of American Growth: The U.S. Standard of Living since the Civil War*, over the course of the nineteenth century, an ice trade developed that involved the large-scale harvesting, transport, and sale of ice. Originally a luxury good, ice enabled the transport of meat in railway cars, supporting the development of Chicago as a meat processing centre and enabling fruits and vegetables to be transported across the country. According to Gordon, as much as one-half of the improvement in nutrition in the 1890s might have been directly attributable to refrigeration. To understand the potential pathways of a transition to a more sustainable society, it is useful to consider the history of the Industrial Revolution. Karl Polanyi, in his 1944 tome, *The Great Transformation*, demonstrated that the Industrial Revolution was not the result of self-regulating markets and that governments played a critical role supporting transformation. Eminent economists Nathan Rosenberg and L.E Birdzell introduced the concept of "gradualness" in *How the West Grew Rich* to describe the day-to-day changes that occur in a time of change. Understanding the dynamics of transitions is important to understand how policy interventions can support finance for sustainable development. Transitions do not have a fixed starting date. In the case of a transition to sustainable economy and society, many of the technologies that will support transition have been in development for decades. The role of government in economic transitions is of particular importance to understanding the power of flow to finance sustainable development. In our modern world, we tend to think of the economy as about either government or the private sector. The reality is that economic transitions involve governments. Finance for all therefore requires both the private sector and governments to play roles at different times. The mass production of the Model T Ford would not have got far if there were no roads to travel on. Coca Cola would not have been able to transport its 'secret sauce' around the United States to bottlers that distributed to customers without investments in railways and municipal water that required approval of governments. Governments can either block or encourage a transition. The same is the case for financial systems. For financial system participants, the way innovation works is poorly understood. This is because the short-term alignment of investors does not align with the long-term nature of economic transitions. The reality of innovation is that it requires persistence. For flow of finance to all there is a need to develop strategies based on an understanding of long-term trends coupled with persistence to establish the companies for tomorrow. There are times in an economic transition when it is difficult to see if flow is making a difference. At some point a trickle of innovation turns into a current that has the potential if encouraged by both governments and financial system participants to become a river. Two quotes sum up the impact of flow on economic transition. Mark Twain when asked how he went bankrupt replied, "Two ways. Gradually, and then suddenly." Nassim Nicholas Taleb's argument in *The Black Swan* was that history does not crawl, it jumps. Flow of finance is necessary for economic transitions. Once a transition starts, it has transformative impacts that could not be imagined when the tap was first opened. To maximize the opportunity to flow finance to all, including supporting economic transitions, there is a need to establish the impact regulatory frameworks that support all forms of finance, not just financialized products.

WHEN FLOW BREAKS DOWN

The Mayan civilization located on the Yucatan Peninsula, which covers parts of mod-ern-day Guatemala, Mexico, Honduras, and El Salvador lasted three thousand years through its sophisticated agriculture system. Around 900 CE several factors, including a long drought that cut off drinking water supplies, contributed to the collapse of the society. In Mesopotamia, the Akkadian Empire covering modern Iran, Saudi Arabia, Bahrain and Oman, which had thrived due to its development of irrigation collapsed due to what scientists attribute to a 300-year-long drought.[38] Angkor, the ancient Khmer empire in Cambodia is believed to have collapsed after monsoon rains flooded its canal, collapsing its infrastructure, which was followed by drought.[39],[40] Just as ancient societies built the systems to enable flow of water and trade, there have been times in history when the flow simply stopped. And the result was the collapse of civilizations.

The Global Financial Crisis, and more recently COVID-19, has illustrated just how fragile system resilience is at times. A "back of the envelope" estimate of the number of people worldwide responsible for the global financial crash. With the simplest of assumptions for 200 countries worldwide, factoring in guesstimates of the numbers of politicians, policymakers, bankers, investors, insurers, professional services firms, and other actors along the investment chain, a core figure of roughly 1.6 million people were culpable for the crash and its impacts.

Sitting alone in a steak restaurant on Columbus Circle in New York, Paul Clements Hunt used this back of the envelop figure as motivation for engagement within the UN[41]. As the world grappled with the Global Financial Crisis, the report, *Lenses and Clocks: Financial stability and systemic risk*[42], argued that to achieve sustainable global growth, wealth creation and poverty reduction, globalization had to become a force for good. asked, "When would we know that our financial system is fit for purpose to deliver a sustainable global economy in the twenty-first century?" In a globalizing marketplace where vast, complex, and powerful financial institutions play a crucial role in a borderless, deregulated, and privatizing world, the report argued that correlation of risk within and among institutions can intensify while remaining hidden. Beyond the financial markets crisis that was caused by factors that financial systems had the power to control, it was argued that a broader range of systemic risks may, in time, also jeopardize economic, social, and financial stability to varying degrees. Resource scarcity, climate change, threats to biodiversity and ecosystems, the demographics of aging populations, and the impact of chronic diseases were identified as prominent examples of a growing list of risks that may threaten the stability of economic and financial systems. A key issue recognized in *Lenses and Clocks* was the need for financial systems to develop new structures and systems to account for and manage emerging risks. A properly functioning and well supervised free market it was argued can also identify, assess, account for and price systemic risks—the so-called "slow failures or creeping risks" that are longer-term in nature. The paper stated, "When approached from a systemic and long-term standpoint, the linkages between financial stability and issues of broader systemic risk, fiduciary legal concerns and the governance of systems and institution are clear. It would appear intuitive that stability in a complex global financial system requires a sound understanding of both short- and long-term risks, demands fiduciaries take full account of such risks when managing capital held in trust, and needs to be underpinned by effective macro and micro governance structures to keep systems and institutions in balance. However, the nature of the linkages between financial system stability and environmental and social risk issues, many longer-term in nature, are not so apparent or quantifiable when viewed over the short term and this is the reason why so many actors along the investment chain simply discount these considerations when dealing in a market with an increasingly short-term perspective". The connection between financial systems and the needs of last mile communities was specifically recognized in the report. "How can the sector work to support the evolution and growth of financial service institutions that—through the market—serve broader environmental and social missions including cooperative activities that address financial exclusion, as well as microfinance, microcredit and micro-insurance services that support financial activity for the base of the pyramid?" The report proposed that financial system participants, "Build a deeper understanding of how policymakers, market regulators and international financing institutions can support the growth and mainstreaming of responsible investment and inclusive finance approaches. Examine, identify, assess and replicate how innovative approaches can be scaled and accelerated to have a direct impact on meeting basic needs and supporting sustainability." Ten years on from the global financial crisis, COVID-19 has demonstrated that system issues are indeed financial issues. COVID-19 itself certainly cannot be described as a black swan event. There were plenty of previous warnings on the dangers of pandemics. The World Health Organization (WHO) through its Global Influenza Surveillance and Response System network, constantly monitored the emergence and evolution of influenza viruses with pandemic potential. WHO argued in its 2015 update that "nothing about influenza is predictable, including where the next pandemic might emerge and which virus might be responsible." Despite the avalanche of information available on pandemic risks, financial system participants were not actively engaged on the issue with only a few individual and institutional exceptions. This is not to cast aspersion on individual organizations but simply reflects the reality of the way system issues are being managed across the global financial system. As the world continues to struggle to manage the consequences of COVID-19 we continue to talk about system risk. There is an evolving understanding of the creeping nature of risk. As the Inter-agency Task Force on Financing for Development's 2021 report on Financing for Sustainable Development stated,[43] "Disasters are often the result of decades of accumulation of risk within social, economic, financial, environmental, and political systems. Risk drivers that have not been sufficiently addressed, such as high debt and excess leverage, poverty and inequality, infrastructure that is not resilient, and climate change, will continue to derail the financing and progress of sustainable development goals (SDGs)". Why is it that we can talk about system risk, but not act? Niall Ferguson in his book *Doom: The Politics of Catastrophe* states, "Disaster takes too many forms for us to process with conventional approaches to risk mitigation. No sooner have we focused our minds on the threat of Salafi jihad than we find ourselves in a financial crisis originating in sub-prime mortgages. No sooner have we relearned that such economic shocks often lead to populist political backlashes than a novel coronavirus is wreaking havoc. What will be next? We cannot know. For every potential calamity, there is at least one possible Cassandra. Not all prophecies can be heeded".[44] Whilst climate change is a clear risk, as Ferguson argues, "In recent years we have allowed one risk—namely climate change—to draw our attention away from others." Ferguson states, "I see the dangers arising from climbing global temperatures as real and potentially catastrophic, but climate change cannot be the sole threat we prepare for".[45] Renowned psychologist Mihaly Csikszentmihályi's argument is that humans have a limit on how much information they can take in. John Naisbitt, the author of the term 'megatrends', built this insight into a business. He argued that "societies, like individuals, can handle only so many concerns at a time".[46] In the 1980's, Naisbitt analysed trends by examining newspaper articles. Because newspapers were at that time a closed system with only so much physical space in a newspaper, a new issue had to compete with existing issues for coverage. By counting articles in newspapers Naisbitt developed a business around advising on developing trends. In combination, the insights of Ferguson, Csikszentmihályi and Naisbitt are relevant to why it is that system risks are not given the consideration within financial systems that they deserve. If system risks take many forms, and if we have limits on what we as humans can focus on, how can we make progress? One answer is to translate the science that lies behind systemic risks into personal narratives. Whenever the dangers of system risks are being debated, there is a need to communicate what it means from a personal perspective. As an example, an increase in global temperatures of 1.5° C is a global average. It is not the increase in temperature across land mass, nor the extreme temperature on a hot summer's day when temperatures in parts of the world have hit 50° C. A rise of 1.5° C tells us nothing about the extreme weather events that will flow from rising temperatures. The reality is that financial systems do many things very well and finance professionals often feel more comfortable with numbers than emotional narratives. To drive change though there is a need for the technical science and numbers to connect to the narrative. Communicating system risk in a number, no matter how large that number may be, will not by itself convince a financial system participant (including government regulators) to make change, that is disruptive to their day-to-day operations, but which is essential to open the flow of finance for all.

A world deprived of the flow of finance is a world in which system risks increase. The mutually reinforcing systems that support the flow of capital into the world's largest financial markets enable those who work in financial institutions to live in what can only be described as comparative luxury. The purpose of this book is not to focus on the excesses that have resulted from bonus cultures to executives in financial institutions and corporations. Plenty of others have ploughed this ground and proposed reforms to curtail the worst excesses. Our focus is on the cost that is born by those that are deprived a flow of finance. Our key point is that "droughts of capital" lead to a loss of system resilience and increase the likelihood of systemic crises.

WHEN FLOW BECOMES A TRICKLE

The peoples living in the cradles of civilization in Mesopotamia, Egypt, China, and India may have been great at building canals but that did not mean water flowed in perpetuity. Around 1,900 BCE Senusret III built a canal from the Nile to the Red Sea. A statue of Ramses II says he either finished or repaired a canal from the Nile to the Red Sea, yet 600 years later Necho II was excavating to build a canal again. Darius the Great constructed a canal but by the time of Cleopatra it was no longer functioning.[47] The flow of water that brought life and sustenance, also contained the silt the ultimately clogs the canal.

As finance flows through an economy, it also contains silt that clogs the system. It is easy to see when there is no flow. It is harder to pinpoint at what point in a canal, tunnel, or pipe where there may be a blockage. As discussed in earlier chapters, structural issues impede the flow of finance to all. These include the rules around investment processes that have the impact, whether intentional or not, of driving behaviours in certain ways. The adherence to Modern Portfolio Theory with its emphasis on minimizing the cost of investment by investing passively is an example of this. With structural impediments, it is at least possible to identify them and examine the ways in which they create problems, and in so doing design solutions. Silt in the financial system is in some ways a deeper more invisible problem. Like silt in water, silt in a financial system consists of many small impediments that collectively grow to become a bigger problem. A single grain of sand is not a problem. Millions and billions of grains of sand are.

Silt in this analogy represents the human capital of a financial system. There are thousands and thousands of people working in financial systems around the world that are fundamentally motivated to do a good job in the best interests of their clients and customers. Yet, financial systems continue to experience scandals. This is not a new phenomenon. The crashing of the South Sea Bubble in 1720 is an example, which should be compulsory reading today. The South Sea Company with its official government links to the Atlantic Slave Trade led to the development of so-called bubble companies. Whilst a satire, the famous line of company seeking capital as "a company for carrying out an undertaking of great advantage, but nobody to know what it is" describes the absurdity of the South Sea boom. Without the inherent greed of individuals, the proponents of bubble companies would not have been able to ply their trade.

There are many examples of silt in a financial system. Some are less than subtle, such as the lobbying efforts in the mid-late 1990's by the Global Climate Coalition (GCC) and The Climate Council (TCC), which operated through a simple playbook of distract, disrupt, delay, question credibility of climate advocates, delay, deny, delay, repeated ad infinitum ad nauseam (which is still going on). Paul Clements Hunt, who as a reporter and Antarctic obsessive followed negotiations from November 1990 at the first session to negotiate the Environmental Protection Protocol for the 1959 Antarctic Treaty to the signing of the Madrid Protocol in October 1991, describes that he was enroute in late 1991 to join a Greenpeace boat as a journalist for the summer season but only got as far as Bangkok where he stayed for seven years. He personally witnessed the lobbying attempts to influence the protocol with the lobbying to protect the ability for minerals and oil exploration a fascinating sub-plot. The period 2041-48 will be critical to ensure Antarctica stays protected as the Treaty/Protocol comes up for renewal fifty years after it came into force in 1998. One of the elements of silt in a financial system are human capital practices that discourage change. As head of United Nations Environment Programme Finance Initiative (UNEP FI) in 2011 Paul was targeted by a major investment bank and asked to join a job recruitment process for a senior executive position. Sitting in their London office for a final interview with a cup of tea, served in the most delicate bone china, Paul's last question was: "What is the biggest risk to the bank?" The single, very senior interviewer and confident of the CEO replied: "Employing an outsider like you." Paul said: "Thanks for the tea," and left.

How do human capital practices create a culture that has led to so many scandals? There is a definite element of behavioural psychology at play. An example witnessed by Paul Clements Hunt in the basement of the Steigenberger Hotel very late one night at the World Economic Forum in Davos was a bash for clients and staff. Messianic, tribal, cultish in that suitably and coolly clad middle-aged, mainly white men way. Partners, bestrode a small stage, seemingly lifted off the ground by hundreds of the most beautiful and richly clad disciples (youngish staff interns). The base beat, thumping vertical lift of the pre-COVID packed crowd felt primeval with the aspirant Partners worshipping at the altar of those who had made it. The sad thing was the men on the stage (and they were all men) looked like clichéd, almost Monty Pythonesque accountants. The simple thought: "This cannot be right." The firm hosting the event and swirling vast amounts of money in one of the most expensive towns on earth was at that time managing a series of scandals.

Efforts to drive change within financial institutions are often subtly undermined. An example is that the mainstreaming of environmental, social and governance (ESG) investment practices has given rise to critiques that are given undue prominence. An interesting case study is of Tariq Fancy, the former head of sustainability investing for the gargantuan asset manager BlackRock, who caused a stir within the investment community when he told *USA Today*: "In truth, sustainable investing boils down to little more than marketing hype, PR spin and disingenuous promises from the investment community". Without judging anyone's motivations Tariq, and those of similar ilk, by seeking to reduce ESG and sustainable finance to a 'marketing' initiative is a way of trying to reduce its influence in an organization and across a financial system. The story of the development of ESG itself has a very real human side. In 2004-2005 a small reprobate group of United Nations officials, and interns, led by Paul Clements Hunt, coined the phrase ESG. At heart, the team was searching for a simple way to engage mainstream finance and investment going beyond SRI (Socially Responsible Investment) and CSR (Corporate Social Responsibility) and needed a term, connected to materiality and fiduciary duty that over time would get traction. Some fifteen to sixteen years on ESG is in vogue and is the toast of the mainstream investment community. The UN Principles for Responsible Investment (PRI), also conceived, driven, and launched (2003-2006) by UNEP Finance Initiative, is now backed by USD 120 trillion in assets and four thousand plus institutional investors. The success of the PRI is a signal that something about ESG, post 2007-2008 financial crash and the 2020-2021 COVID-19 Pandemic, and the unfolding systemic horror of climate and ecosystems destructions, resonates and is taking hold worldwide. The wind has shifted for multiple reasons and ESG thinking helped that shift. The reality of ESG is that it threatened, and threatens, what has been a very cosy financial world. For many years, there was no doubt that mainstream finance professionals did their best to ignore ESG. It is arguable that this was an advantage to emerging ESG practitioners who were able to gain a foothold on the inside of the financial system. As a result, ESG principles are now ingrained into the operations of institutional investors through investment policies and are now legitimized by central banks and financial system regulators who are embodying ESG into their own regulatory practices. This is of critical importance. The locking of ESG into regulatory practices provides a foundation through which finance can flow to all. The Tariq Fancy case study recalls former US President Theodore Roosevelt's April 1910 speech in Paris: "The poorest way to face life is to face it with a sneer," he said. "A cynical habit of thought and speech, a readiness to criticize work which the critic himself never tries to perform, an intellectual aloofness which will not accept contact with life's realities—all these are marks, not ... of superiority but of weakness." Roosevelt then delivered his much quoted but worth repeating passage: "It is not the critic who counts; not the man who points out how the strong man stumbles, or where the doer of deeds could have done them better. The credit belongs to the man who is actually in the arena, whose face is marred by dust and sweat and blood; who strives valiantly; who errs, who comes short again and again, because there is no effort without error and shortcoming; but who does actually strive to do the deeds; who knows great enthusiasms, the great devotions; who spends himself in a worthy cause; who at the best knows in the end the triumph of high achievement, and who at the worst, if he fails, at least fails while daring greatly, so that his place shall never be with those cold and timid souls who neither know victory nor defeat."

In the context of finance for all, silt in a financial system is the mutually reinforcing practices leading to system risks that result in the accumulation of capital into a small number of massive pools, which in turn create monopoly-like conditions for institutional investment managers and the conditions for excessive executive pay and corporate bonuses. Because the factors that support accumulation of capital by a small group of firms remain in place, with more capital constantly being added to the existing deep pools of capital by pension funds and sovereign wealth funds, unless there is intervention, we will continue to see excessive lifestyles that result from these monopoly-like conditions. By contrast to the monopoly-like conditions that are supporting the flow of capital to the deepest pools, the rest of the world is being starved of capital. An implication of modern institutional investment practices is that as capital flows to a handful of stock exchanges, other stock exchanges are being deprived of capital. If not resolved, we will continue to see a distortion of both the economies where capital flows to, and the economies where it does not. The continuation, and exacerbation of global imbalances will in turn create system risks.

The focus on the development of ESG by UNEP FI and other individuals and organizations over the last twenty years reflected the dominance of financial institutions in driving the regulation of financial systems. To address the accumulation of silt in financial institutions that acts to impede new ways of thinking, one of the challenges that must be addressed is path dependency. Path dependency is a term that describes a situation where what has occurred in the past persists because of resistance to change. In *The Power of Creative Destruction: Economic Upheaval and the Wealth of Nations*, the authors examine the impact of path dependency on green innovation and find that the probability that a firm would produce a green patent increased by 5 percent if more than 10 percent of its past patents were green. "A firm that has registered more polluting patents in the past has a higher probability of producing a polluting patent today."[48] The argument is that the past direction of a firm influences their future direction. To alter the path dependency of a financial institution, and indeed a financial system, there is a need for interventions that prevent existing practices being repeated. Financial System Impact Regulation is a term that we use to describe regulatory practices that removes "silt" to ensure the ongoing health of a financial system and financial institutions. Up until now financial system regulators have largely played a passive role when it comes to sustainable development. It is arguable that this changed in 2021. Amongst all the changes we collectively witnessed in what was a turbulent year, the changes that took place to embed climate-related financial risks into the supervisory practices of financial system regulators and standard setters are perhaps the least examined and understood. Whilst over the course of 2021 attention on climate change was naturally drawn to Glasgow and COP26, the rules of the global financial system were being quietly re-written to lock-in consideration of climate change in finance practices. The process of change began innocuously enough. On January 25, 2021, just a couple of weeks after the confirmation of President Biden, the Federal Reserve Bank of New York announced that Kevin Stiroh had been appointed to lead a Board of Governors on Climate.[49] The Federal Reserve then announced on March 23, 2021, that it was establishing a Financial Stability Climate Committee (FSCC) to identify, assess, and address climate-related risks to financial stability.[50] By the end of the year the powerful Financial Stability Oversight Council (FSOC), which was established as part of the Dodd-Frank Wall Street Reform and Consumer Protection Act, had issued its Report on Climate-Related Financial Risk.[51]

Internationally as the Italian Government prepared to host the G20, a largely unknown study group on sustainable finance was transformed to become the G20 Sustainable Finance Working Group.[52] This was no ordinary working group. Its members, including the Bank of International Settlements (BIS), Financial Stability Board (FSB), Organization for Economic Co-operation and Development (OECD), World Bank, and the International Organization of Securities Commissions (IOSCO), effectively govern the global financial system. What has been largely underappreciated is that the working group was (and still is) co-chaired by China and the United States. In the lead-up to COP26, the G20 SFWG produced its Sustainable Finance Roadmap, which was endorsed by G20 finance ministers and central bank governors on October 7, 2021. The roadmap outlined a pathway on how the G20 will embed climate change into the activities of financial system regulators and standard setters. Up until now the approach of international financial system regulators on climate change could be characterized by the lack of coordination. The way to describe the G20 SFWG is that it is the 'one ring to bind them all'. Importantly, the Roadmap committed the SFWG to produce a Synthesis Report, which will report on progress each year. The appendixes of the roadmap outline in detail the activities that will take place over the next few years and which agency will be responsible for driving them. Two significant developments are the support by financial system regulators for the establishment of the International Sustainability Standards Board (ISSB) and the release by the Basel Committee on Banking Supervision of the draft "Principles for the effective management and supervision of climate-related financial risks", which was released on November 16, 2021. There is no doubt that the drive to integrate climate-related financial risks into financial system regulation has been coming out of the United States. The EU was already active in this space, but until the US engaged its efforts have struggled to gain momentum. One explanation as to why the US is moving so fast is the volatility of US politics. If climate-related risk management is locked into international financial system regulation, then this is one way to ensure that momentum on climate change continues whatever happens in future

Presidential elections. The implication for financing sustainable development is that consideration of climate change is shifting from a voluntary to a compulsory activity. ESG practices have largely been developed outside of government. In fact, it is arguable that one reason why ESG achieved such dominance as an investor paradigm is because regulators largely left it alone. The reality is that whilst investors control what they invest in, it is financial system regulators that establish the frameworks within which investment takes place. An analogy is the building of a canal. It can take a while for the engineers to work out where to build. During the time taken to construct a canal it is easy to question whether the canal will have impact. But once the canal is built and is operational, the flow of water is unstoppable. The activity of financial system regulators over the coming decade will have significant implications and create opportunities for finance to flow to all. The developments that took place in 2021 should be seen in a historic context. As discussed, earlier in the book, the *Domesday Book*, compiled in 1086, recorded sixty market towns. Historically, it was governments that directed the formation of market towns and regulated activities within them. Governments have always had a critical role to play in creating the market environments that open a flow of finance for all. To go back to our ancient canal analogy, the decision that Necho II faced whether to repair or build a canal to the Red Sea would have required the same expense of time and resources. In our modern financial system, focusing efforts on repairing the existing financial system to improve the flow of finance to all makes sense and in practical terms is the only course of action. A focus on Financial System Impact Regulation is one mechanism through which a finance system can be kept free of silt and open the flow of finance for all.

THE FLOW OF IDEAS

The annual flood of the Nile determined whether there was feast or famine in ancient Egypt. The Egyptians built nilometers to measure the strength of the flood. There were different types of nilometre, which essentially consisted of a column that was strategically placed to measure the annual flood level. A low level on the nilometer indicated that there would not be enough food. If the nilometer was high, it indicated that the flood would be destructive. The Egyptians system of nilometers supported the calculation of taxes and developed measuring units, which advanced mathematics. Historical nilometer data is today used as a source of climate data.[53]

We began our flow journey in the Turkish city of Gaziantep where we described how the network of caravanserai on the Persian Royal Road and Silk Road were not just roadside inns where travellers could rest but were significant pieces of infrastructure that were built and maintained to facilitate trade. The name caravanserai consists of two words: Caravan (group of travellers) and Seray (house and place to stay) and means House for group of travellers.[54] UNESCO states: "*The long-standing and ongoing legacy of this remarkable network is reflected in the many distinct but interconnected cultures, languages, customs and religions that have developed and spread over millennia along these routes. The passage of merchants and travellers of many different nationalities resulted not only in commercial exchange but in a continuous and widespread process of cultural interaction. As such, from their early, exploratory origins, the Silk Roads developed to become a driving force in the formation of diverse societies across Eurasia and far beyond*". Caravanserai were places where different cultures engaged with each other.

The result was not just exchange of goods, but transmission of ideas. Two transformative innovations that travelled through the Silk Road were paper and the waterwheel. The Noria irrigation waterwheel invented in Syria was used as widely as Spain to the Yellow River in China.[55]

Discussions around sustainability often focus on how much finance is needed to achieve a particular outcome. Figures are bandied about to the point that they become meaningless. Just as the ancient Egyptians measured the actual flow of the Nile, there a need to focus on measuring the amount of flow that is *received*. A starting point to measure financial system flow for all is to understand where we are at today. Climate change is an obvious place to focus. A relative measure of financial flow to climate change are investments made by investment funds, insurance corporations and pension funds (ICPFs). According to data from the European Central Bank (ECB), ICPFs invest "around €1.3 trillion and €0.3 trillion respectively in securities issued by high emitters operating mainly in the industrial, energy and materials sectors. While the relative share of high-emitting firms in non-banks' portfolios has remained broadly stable at around 30% over the last seven years, the absolute amount has doubled, from €0.8 trillion in 2013 to €1.6 trillion in 2019, broadly in line with the growth of non-bank assets".[56] ECB's data tells us that despite the focus on climate change by financial system participants, institutional investment portfolios have not shifted. In absolute terms, financial systems are in fact continuing to tip more money into high-emitting industries. This gives as a starting point, at least for financial flow into high-emitting industries. The relative rate of financial flow away from high-emitting industries is zero. This of course doesn't tell us the whole story. Over the last twenty-five years there has been a significant focus by financial system participants on sustainable development with some notable improvements in practices. But it does give us an absolute measure to assess whether the extent to which the gradual introduction of new practices is leading to measurable outcomes. Going back to the water flow analogy, the flow of water through a canal, pipe, or hose, is the last point of a cycle that started with the building of the necessary infrastructure to enable flow. In the case of water, societies devoted significant time and resources to build enabling infrastructure. Finishing the job of building infrastructure was itself a cause for celebration. An example is New York's Croton Aqueduct, which was completed in 1842, bringing fresh water to New York's growing population that literally transformed people's lives. To celebrate the completion of the aqueduct the city built the iconic Bethesda Fountain in Central Park, which is topped by the Angel of the Waters. The journey from idea to implementation though was not an easy one. New York in the 1830's was still a swampy woodland. The inability to access clean water severely impacted the city's development and resulted in ongoing health issues for the population. In the month of July 1832 alone, two thousand New Yorkers died from an outbreak of Asiatic cholera with more than three thousand five hundred deaths that year. More than eighty thousand people fled the city because of the cholera outbreak. The outbreak of cholera it is arguable was a turning point for the population.[57] A proposal by the city's Board of Health was made to access water from the Croton River forty miles away. In the past, the idea had been dismissed as too expensive but in April 1835 the question to build the Croton Aqueduct was put to the people of New York with overwhelming support for the proposal. The next seven years would prove to be traumatic for New Yorkers. The Great Fire of 1835 destroyed nearly 700 buildings. In 1836 and 1837, wheat crops suffered from disease, which led to an increase in the price of wheat. New Yorkers rioted in February 1837 after concerns that flour was being hoarded by speculators.[58] An increase in interest rates from the Bank of England flowed through the banks in America leading to the Panic of 1837 with 343 of the 850 banks in the United States closing, resulting in a depression. Despite all these events the construction on the Croton Aqueduct continued and on June 27, 1842, water flowed for the first time from the Croton River to Manhattan. Population subsequently increased and by the 1880's more than one million people lived in New York.

The challenge with building a canal is that until the water flows it is difficult to get a true measure of the impact of the progress that has been made. This is particularly important when it comes to understanding the transformative impact of ideas. The development and implementation of good ideas is critical to the flow of finance for all. Ideas take time to mature and to be implemented. Ideas require a safe place for honest and open dialogue. As Paul Krugman says, "new ideas should be judged as ideas, not by whether those proposing those ideas talk a good game".[59] The United Nations has itself played a critical role facilitating discussion on new ideas on the role that finance can play to support sustainable development. It is arguable that the starting point of the global financial system's focus on sustainable development goes back to 1983 when the UN Secretary General Javier Pérez de Cuéllar, after an affirmation by the UN General Assembly, commissioned the former Prime Minister of Norway, Gro Harlem Brundtland to create a Commission independent of the UN to focus on environmental and developmental problems. The Brundtland Commission is today perhaps best known for the definition of sustainability, arguing that "humanity has the ability to make development sustainable to ensure that it meets the needs of the present without compromising the ability of future generations to meet their own needs". The report itself also introduced the concept of "interlocking crises" as it considered the challenge of sustainable development in the context of an African drought that put 36 million people at risk; a leak from a pesticides factory in Bhopal, India that killed more than two thousand people; an explosion of liquid gas tanks in Mexico City that killed thousand people; the Chernobyl nuclear reactor explosion that sent nuclear fallout across Europe; and agricultural chemicals, solvents, and mercury flowing into the Rhine River during a warehouse fire in Switzerland, killing millions of fish and threatening drinking water in the Federal Republic of Germany and the Netherlands. The Brundtland Commission opened-up a global discussion on sustainable development that has progressed in multiple forms over the last thirty-five years. The Commission was followed by the United Nations Conference on Environment and Development (Earth Summit) that was held in Rio de Janeiro, Brazil in June 1992. From the perspective of financial systems, the Brundtland Commission can also be traced back as the foundation of a dialogue that ultimately led to the establishment of the United Nations Environment Program Finance Initiative (UNEP FI) in the lead-up to the Earth Summit.[60]

When it comes to the transmission of ideas, why is UNEP FI special? Paul Clements-Hunt headed UNEP FI as a UN Official from November 2000-March 2012 and is well placed to provide his own personal insights into the unique set of dynamics that existed. Paul says "In my mind UNEP FI's real role was to mobilize capital and finance at massive scale to support sustainable development globally. I never bought the idea that as the partnership was between banks, insurers and investors with UNEP, the UN's environmental arm, our focus should only be green finance. As head of UNEP FI, I drove my growing team to dive headfirst into the environmental, social, and systemic governance challenges of a financial sector riding high, until the crash of 2007-8 that is, on the bounties of globalisation in an era of deregulation and liberalized markets following the US Goldilocks economy of the 1990s. I came to learn first-hand the immense opportunities which well-engineered UN-private sector collaboration could deliver, the inevitable tensions catalysed by very "different beasts", and, in some cases, the downright contempt parts of the UN and parts of the private sector had for each other. I always felt I was managing the ultimate clash of cultures. There were brilliant, inspiring people on each side, UN and private, trying to find a way to meaningful partnership. Others felt the UN had sold "the iconic badge" cheaply to rapacious private financial institutions for branding purposes and the most judgemental private executives castigated the UN as an utterly useless "no action" bureaucracy despite what they professed in public". Prior to the UNEP FI, the UN had a mixed history in terms of relationships with the private sector. The history of UN-private sector relations dates to the very earliest days of the august multi-lateral organisation. The Paris-based International Chamber of Commerce (ICC)[61], was the only private organisation accredited to the 1945 International Conference for Organization (ICO) which created the UN Charter as the world emerged from six years of catastrophic war in which 60 million died. Building on its attendance at the ICO during the war, ICC became one of the very early, if not the first, non-government organisations (NGO) to be given "top level consultative status" to the UN in 1946. ICC finally gained full observer status to the UN in 2016. Paul continues, "And then? The "geopolitical breaks" were hit very hard. The options for deep collaboration between the UN and the private sector disappeared overnight and did not surface for nearly 50 years. Why? Prospective UN partnerships with the private sector were de-railed by intensifying Cold War ideology where free market views collided with statist thinking around socio-economic growth. In the polarized world between 1946-1991, where largely the Member Governments of the UN adhered to either capitalism or communism, with various shades in between, UN engagement with the private sector was curtailed in the extreme". The relevance of the Cold War on UN private sector relationships is relevant today as an unimaginable war rages between two European powers with the global financial system and financial sector in upheaval after happily doing business with, financing, and investing in the economy of a malevolent autocracy turned aggressive nationalist invader whose mask, only lightly fixed on at any stage, has slipped off completely. Paul describes how the melting of the Cold War led to a breakthrough. "A meeting in New York between the then Executive Secretary of UNEP, Mostafa Tolba, with 28 banks was the catalyst for the partnership between the UN and the beating heart of both the 'red in tooth and claw capitalism' global financial sector. Just months after the Cold War ended the UN engaged with, in the first place, banks, followed by insurers and investors, to build an enduring partnership which turned 30 years old on 27th May 2022. The partnership was set in place by Tolba, a wily and astute Egyptian diplomat, immediately ahead of the ground-breaking United Nations Conference on Environment and Development (UNCED), better known as the 1992 Rio Earth Summit which saw the world's leaders gather in Brazil for the first time collectively to discuss sustainable development in the immediate aftermath of the Cold War". Was UNEP FI a smooth history of UN-private partnership? No. A productive one? Paul says "I would argue yes to a degree, as without UNEP FI, amongst other things, we would not have the August 2004 coined concept of ESG (environmental, social and governance) nor the UN-supported Principles for Responsible Investment (UNPRI) launched by the late UNSG Kofi Annan at the New York Stock Exchange in April 2006. UNEP FI's greatest achievement, in my opinion, is unheralded and often over-looked. It was the development and roll out from 2005-2022 of the UNEP FI Environmental Social Risk Analysis (ESRA) training course. ESRA has taken more than 3,000 bankers, possibly far more, through a deep dive look at why and how this broad basket of environmental and social issues are critical to the future of banking, finance and the broader investment chain going forward. For me ESRA is UNEP FI's equivalent of the beat of the wings of a butterfly creating great change across the financial world. So, yes, UNEP FI is special as a partnership sparked as the Cold War ended and re-opening the potential of UN-private partnerships after a break of 46 years".

Over the course of thirty years UNEP FI's partnership with the financial system has created a series of initiatives including founding the Principles for Responsible Investment (PRI), Principles for Responsible Banking (PRB), the Principles for Sustainable Insurance (PSI) and the Natural Capital Declaration. PRI itself is now backed by 4,500 plus investors globally representing US$ 83 trillion in assets with a team of close to 200 staff in London. The power of UNEP FI was that it created an umbrella for a geographically diverse financial services sector to come together to discuss ideas that would have been difficult to discuss within an individual financial institution. Over the course of its history UNEP FI has produced hundreds of reports with collaboration involving thousands of individuals. Perhaps the key benefit of UNEP FI's working groups was that they were off the radar off from the mainstream conversations that were taking place at the time. This allowed a group of individuals to network and organize and to collectively build ideas that ultimately framed actions across the global financial system. An example is UNEP Finance Initiative's "Values to Value (V2V)" report[62] released in 2004. The report stated, "If V2V has one core message it is this: sustainability, built into the governance and operational mechanisms of financial institutions and capital markets, can become a powerful driver that rebuilds ecological integrity, deepens our social fabric, and guarantees a responsible approach to business based on sound values". The objective of the V2V report was to encourage and assist financial institutions—whatever their size and wherever they operate in the world—to adapt their activities to support the goals of sustainable development. The report promoted the idea that, "financial institutions which seek to realize the 'People, Planet, Prosperity' ethic in their operations will become powerful drivers of change for the benefit of the environment and of the communities in which they operate". An important part of UNEP FI's work was to focus on addressing impediments to the integration of environment, social and governance (ESG) factors into financial decision-making processes. An example of this was the focus by UNEP FI's Asset Management Working Group (AMWG) on fiduciary duty. In 2005, Freshfields Bruckhaus Deringer was commissioned to provide an expert opinion "on the question whether the law restricts us, as asset managers, from seeking to attend to broadly accepted extra-financial interests of savers in conjunction with their financial interests". In commissioning the legal opinion, the UNEP FI's AMWG stated, "What we have in mind are certain social and environmental interests that find expression in diverse international treaties, norms, and declarations, particularly those emerging from the democratic deliberative processes of the United Nations. Furthermore, we have also asked whether fiduciary duty does not require us to take into account such considerations, in view of their materiality to equity pricing." The resulting landmark "Freshfields" report produced by Professor Paul Watchman, a former Partner at Freshfields stated:[63] "In our view, decision-makers are required to have regard (at some level) to ESG considerations in every decision they make. This is because there is a body of credible evidence demonstrating that such considerations often have a role to play in the proper analysis of investment value. As such they cannot be ignored, because doing so may result in investments being given an inappropriate value". The importance of the Freshfields report was to provide a legal backing, which enabled fiduciary investors such as pension funds to become signatories to the Principles for Responsible Investment (PRI). PRI was formally launched by United Nations Secretary General Kofi Annan on April 27, 2006, at the New York Stock Exchange Opening Bell Ceremony on the Exchange's iconic balcony. This launch demonstrated the potential for the head of the world's multi-lateral system to partner with the globe's most powerful financial institutions. Another important innovation led by UNEP FI was to develop the term ESG that brought together the three critical issues of environment, social and governance. Prior to the use of the term ESG, terms including GES (governance, environment and social) were beginning to be used to describe so called non-financial factors in investment decision-making. The concept behind ESG developed by Paul Clements Hunt and the UNEP FI team, which included Gordon Haggart, Jacob Malthouse Trevor Bowden, James Gifford, Philip Walker and Ken Maguire, was that by putting the "S" for social in the middle it would not be forgotten or flicked off the end of the acronym because social issues were often deemed as the most difficult by investors and businesses. Many investors and corporations would have been delighted to see the troublesome "S" flicked off the end of ESG, a sentiment that continues to this day. Paul says, "It is important to get the origins right as success has many 'Mothers and Fathers' and failure an orphan. The origins of ESG right now are a tad confused ranging from invented by an advertising agency, to being created by academics, to a left wing conspiracy. What I know is that a group of young consultants, interns and a few UN staffers came up with ESG through blood, sweat and tears and through a desire to change the way capital markets engage with the immense systemic risks and opportunities presented by ESG issues. Never could we have imagined that 17 years on ESG would be sweeping along the investment chain, the legal world and throughout the corporate world. Yes, there's a huge ESG bubble, the dangers of greenwash and greenwish are immense and/but like all good things that are true and have a solid anchor as a base, Real ESG will come through, survive, and continue to change billions of lives for the better. A whole host of people who contributed blood, sweat, tears and sacrificed family life and loved ones on the mission's 1st Phase that lasted from April 2003, the initiation of UNEP FI's Asset

Management Working Group (AMWG), to April 27th, 2006, when the late, and truly great UN Secretary General, Kofi Annan, in an iconic moment, opened the US Markets on the iconic balcony at the New York Stock Exchange as he launched the UN Principles for Responsible Investment anchored in ESG thinking. PRI is now backed by 4,500 plus investment institutions and over USD 120 trillion in assets. Impressive? No. But it will be when they are all investing in a true ESG aligned way. It is however one huge signal for the world that these asset owners, managers, and advisors are committed to ESG and on their own journeys. Love, hate or be indifferent about ESG but it has done what we at UNEP FI originally intended: it changed the conversation with finance and investment beyond CSR and ethics to materiality".

Ideas in turn generate partnerships to implement them. Over the last thirty years since the establishment of UNEP FI we have seen a raft of global partnerships sprouting including UNCTAD's Sustainable Stock Exchange Initiative (SSEI started in 2009), the Financial Stability Board's Task Force on Climate-Related Disclosure (TCFD started in 2015) and more recently the Network of Central Banks and Supervisors for Greening the Financial System (NGFS), which is a group of Central Banks and Supervisors working on a voluntary basis, to share best practices and contribute to the development of environment and climate risk practices. As ideas generate partnerships there is a need to remind ourselves of Brundtland's argument that, "in the end, sustainable development is not a fixed state of harmony, but rather a *process of change* in which the exploitation of resources, the direction of investments, the orientation of technological development, and institutional change are made consistent with future as well as present needs". There have been many positive developments since Brundtland began her work in 1983. We would all hope for instance that incidents such as Bhopal will never re-occur. Brundtland's concept that sustainable development is a *process of change* is relevant to the enabling infrastructure that needs to be put in place to support system change. Because sustainable development is indeed a "process of change" the ways and means through which we address sustainable development challenges need to be constantly revisited. The canal is far from complete, and the flow of finance has yet to arrive. It is certainly too early to celebrate. Like the Croton Aqueduct, the canal is being built at a time of turmoil, which leads some people to question whether it has value. The good news though is that over the last thirty years the collaborative foundations have been built that has the potential to enable a flow of finance to all. The question is therefore not how far we have come, but what further actions are needed to open a flow of finance to all. Having examined a range of elements that create, sustain, or inhibit the flow of finance, we now turn to ideas that can support a flow of finance for all.

FLOW AND PARTNERSHIPS

It was a simple coffee table book. The story of the United Nations Headquarter (UNHQ) building in New York City in photos. Flicking through it in late 2008 browsing in the UN book shop in the HQ basement before a late flight from JFK Airport back home to Geneva, Paul Clements Hunt bought it. "I was done, dusted, gone, resignation letter handwritten, and my fury had been building. Not with the UN but with the hundreds of institutions – banks, insurers, investors – which were the core of the partnership between global financial services and United Nations Environment Programme Finance Initiative (UNEP FI). I simply could not reconcile the institutions which, in every public announcement, forward-looking statement on climate change, inequality or sustainability, were those at the heart of the devastating 2007-8 global financial crash crushing families, communities, charities, and businesses worldwide. Worse, I felt as the Head of UNEP FI I'd helped hold a UN blue fig leaf over the incompetence, negligence, greed, and criminality of the whole panoply of financial institutions which had signed up to UNEP FI since 1992. I'd been holding the "fig leaf" for a full eight years after starting as a UN staffer heading the initiative since 2000. Nor could I reconcile the passion, belief, and actions of brilliant executives from, amongst many others, ABN AMRO Banco Real, ABSA, Allianz, AXA, BNP Paribas, Diamond Bank, Barclays, Calvert, Citigroup, Munich Reinsurance, State Street, Swiss Reinsurance, and Tokyo Marine, who believed in every facet of sustainable finance and responsible investment, with what their institutions had committed. Flicking through on the flight home it told in understated terms a wonderful story of resilience, revitalisation, creativity, and collective will not to mention – between the lines - intrigue, skulduggery, and high politics. I was humbled. If a generation which had suffered two world wars over 30 years could come together to create the UN, design, and agree on an iconic UN building, and get to work rebuilding a world clawing its way out of a war that cost 60 million lives, then surely, I could get over the global financial crash? My fervent belief in UN values underpinning a partnership with the global financial services sector were re-ignited".

The use of 'partnerships' to address systemic or cross-sector challenges has become more prolific over the past three decades. What arguably started off as a critical tool in the political management of foreign aid programs or the decline of Europe's post-industrial cities in the 1990's, has now evolved to become a mainstream tool used to create collective agency in managing the politics about change. Not surprisingly therefore the idea of partnership-led responses to the planet's existential threats has resulted in an entire Sustainable Development Goal dedicated to its role and application. SDG17 has created a new momentum and interest in partnership-led responses resulting in the use of partnerships to deliver everything from advocacy through to practical and material changes on the ground. While the value of partnerships and their diversity is not the subject here, it's worth making a distinction between different types of 'partnerships'. Three core types of partnership are identified. We have discussed partnerships that are generated to take forward ideas. The establishment of UNEP FI out of the work of Gro Harlem Brundtland is an example of this. Partnerships may be grounded in public relations, communications, sponsorship, and marketing. It is partnerships that are grounded in design thinking, finance, cross-sector implementation, and venture building that we now turn our attention to. While not mutually exclusive, the latter takes primacy in complex undertakings where vertically integrated 'cross-sector implementation facilities' comprising providers and seekers of capital are required to address humanities wicked problems in a way that is systemic, place-based, and scalable.

Achieving the SDGs is dependent on realizing place-based outcomes at scale. It's that simple. Executing this, however, is slightly more complex not least because it requires us to re-wire the relationship between capital and the economy (from local to supra national) and in so doing create an economic condition that measures success in terms of progress, not growth, towards human and planetary health. While there are numerous variables that require (re)alignment in this transition, there is one principle that is foundational and that is that no one entity can achieve this alone. Achieving local impacts at scale requires an enterprise approach to aligning the right financial, political, and technical scaffolding. Sitting at the heart of this idea are two important conditions, one, that a vertically integrated financial system emerges and two, that a healthy and sustainable global municipal finance marketplace is created. To this end, each of the SDGs from 1 to 16 must be fully investable, financeable, and insurable, with supportive financing platforms based on the standardization and systemization of the key indicators underpinning the goals. Partnerships catalysed by the collaborative sentiments of SDG17, covering governments, public and private finance, and broad civil society, with a focus on creativity will engineer new financial and investment approaches, products, and platforms. Innovation, across every dimension of the financial system, not just the financial sector, will be anchored in creativity, disruptive digital applications, and engineered on an inclusive basis leaving no community behind. Cross-sector implementation facilities and 'partnership building' are the primary mechanism by which public, private and civil sector interests come together to build and scale SDG-aligned ventures (project, program, or business). Cross-Sector Implementation Facilities (CSIF) are partnerships committed to catalysing blended capital into place-based impact through the scaling of fit-for-purpose enterprise structures. Based on the Implementation Facility for Sustainable Urban Development model (IFSUD)[64] that the UN and World Bank Group set out to establish, CSIF's are by their very nature geared towards creating scalable and sustainable cross-sector approaches to financing and implementing SDG-aligned ventures. The objective of the proposed UN – World Bank IFSUD was to catalyse effective, coordinated support to countries and cities towards the common aim of harnessing urbanization as a solution to poverty, inequality, climate change, and other barriers to sustainable development. IFSUD aimed to act as both a catalytic vehicle for transformative investments in urban development, at scale, and a mechanism for cooperative partnership. The intent was to draw together committed partners, relevant stakeholders, and all levels of government, as well as the private sector. But not all 'partnerships' lead to enterprise solutions or form the basis to a genuine implementation facility. In fact, it is important to note that 'partnerships' are not an end in themselves but simply the means through which an appropriate or fit-for-purpose organizational form or implementation facility is developed. Across the broad spectrum of engagement there are many 'partnerships' that might more appropriately be referred to as alliances, collaborations, or reference groups. This is not to say that distinguishing these from 'partnerships' is in any way a rebuttal of their value, quite the opposite, these collectives are critical to advancing advocacy, policy, and agenda planning. However, their composition, commitment and resourcing reflect the specific nature of these outputs and are typically in absence of the stakeholders and influence required to finance and implement change. To this end, 'partnerships' that underpin CSIF's reflect a different commitment to implementation, scale, resourcing, governance, funding, and duration. They can be seen as stand-alone exercises or as part of a sequence of evolving organizational forms and governance towards permanent venture creation. CSIF's reflect three very potent forces coming together. On the one hand, there are private sector skills in commercialization, risk management and fiduciary governance, public sector influence as stewards of assets and control over regulatory and policy levers, and civil sector groups with a long track record in exercising social license. The challenge embodied by the SDG's requires all three to come together in what is sometimes referred to as 4th sector convergence. Accordingly, the process by which 4th sector partnerships or CSIF's are developed also reflect a highly unique undertaking often requiring existing governance, finance and implementation approaches to be dismantled and re-assembled to reflect cross-sector values and alignment. CSIF's have an eye on the horizon beyond transaction, advocacy and planning documents and instead focus on transformation, implementation, and impact. CSIF's are underpinned by three distinct or interrelated partnership typologies; Project Partnerships; Program Partnerships; and/or Business Partnerships. That is to say that each can either be a step in an evolutionary sequence towards fully independent ventures in perpetuity or exist as self-contained exercises with a limited life.

Project Partnerships – Typically employed to test and prototype ideas or deliver one-off initiatives. Decision-making, resourcing, and funding have their origins from within 'parent' partner-organizations and are usually managed by a project control group. Project Partnerships reflect the governance requirements and decision-making timeframes of each partner-organization. These partnership types can be used to pilot or prototype ideas with a view to progressing towards the limited scaling of an idea for a specific community.

Program Partnerships – Typically employed to implement self-contained programs of work or to scale ideas from the prototyping phase. This might also involve opening the partnership to other stakeholders critical to scaling, resourcing, and funding. Typically, this partnership type is characterized by a cross-sector quango-like structure comprising representation from key partner-organizations. The quango is empowered to make decisions on behalf of partner-organizations, and therefore able to progress at a much faster rate. That said, critical liability still resides with the 'parent' partner-organization given that they would typically be responsible for resourcing and funding.

Business Partnerships – This partnership type reflects a considerable investment in time and resources required to develop and test a business model. Assuming the program partnership has succeeded in proving concept at scale, the business partnership might become a self-contained incorporated entity replete with its own governance structure, business model, funding, and associated liabilities.

These partnership types and the process by which they are built position ESG and SDG considerations at the heart of the partnership building process, and therefore is core to the way CSIF operates. CSIF's are characterized by seven building blocks[65] critical to high performance. They are:

- *Sustainable Business Model*: Relationship between business focus, finance/funding and implementation/execution in a way that is sustainable development informed, and SDG aligned.
- *Governance:* Executive direction of the CSIF in a way that is consistent with sustainable development and ESG principles.
- *Operational Management Structure:* Management institution required to implement 'project/program/business' in a way that is consistent with executive direction.
- *Communications Strategy:* Deliberative and effective communication systems critical to building and sustaining sound relationships.
- *Core Competencies:* Implementation requires having the right capability and capacity. Stakeholder Management and Engagement: Critical and evolving process by which stakeholder relationships are consistently revised to reflect their role and stake in the emergence of fit-for-purpose CSIF.
- *Monitoring and Evaluation:* CSIF are contemporary organizational forms and are therefore held to account via the process of 'double materiality' reporting.

A foundation of successful CSIF's is their ability to engage with financial markets and be visible within the financial system. CSIF are distinct from other delivery forms and structures due to their use of blended finance approaches involving 'patient capital' and the pursuit of sustainable change management. In this context, the semantic difference between 'implementation' and 'delivery' is important. The aim of CSIF's whether through projects, programs, and embedded ventures, is to implement and sustain change, an undertaking which is first and foremost a structural and cultural undertaking. Delivering outcomes is typically a technical exercise in execution. The distinction between 'implementation' and 'delivery' also determines where and how CSIF's operate within the financial system and will be discussed later. In today's financialized economy markets are the principal means through which financial systems allocate capital. Markets are also the principal means for finance to support the delivery of the SDGs. The challenge we identify today is that as global financial markets are becoming deeper and deeper, local markets are not benefiting from this strength. Financial markets are both the reservoirs and canals of financial systems. Capital flows into stock exchanges, which then funds businesses. Finance flows through global bond markets. The amount of capital that flows into a stock exchange is a measure of its potential to finance sustainable development. For CSIF's to be more visible, and therefore take advantage of deeper global financial markets they must ensure that the partnership that underpinned them comprise the vertical integration of stakeholders/actors critical to the finance and implementation of a particular project, program, or business. To date, multilateral and supranational policy objectives aimed at localizing SDG's have largely failed to do so at scale. The primary reason for this is that the business of meeting place-based needs has no meaningful presence in the same investment value chain occupied by the UN and other horizontally aligned multilateral, supranational or multinational public and private interests. To put it another way, relying on the trickle-down policy effect is not working and not because the inherent content of policy is not aligned between the UN and say a local authority but because there is no operational line of sight between decision making at the UN level through to local communities. Vertically integrating operations may however provide an answer. The term is not new insofar as its common place to describe a business operation, which owns and controls other upstream or downstream operations/businesses in the same value or supply chain. Many businesses increasingly choose vertical integration as a way of addressing corporate ESG commitments and achieving a form of stewardship of the commons. While stewardship of the commons is typically associated with investment decision making, in the context of corporate strategy, owning operations within the same value or supply chain can improve financial materiality. When seeking to localize SDG's, vertical integration of business or operations along 'an' SDG value/supply chain can similarly improve financial materiality, thereby removing perceived risk-based impediments to the leveraging of development impact. A vertically integrated partnership might typically reflect alignment between those that own capital, regulate capital, activate/catalyse capital, and those for whom the impact is being sought. Building successful cross-sector implementation facilities (CSIF) requires an architecture of 'double materiality' to emerge. This means that on the one hand the implementation facility itself, which through good governance upholds the principles of ESG, exists in a sustainable manner and on the other hand by virtue of its business offering and how it goes about executing that offering has a positive impact on the sustainable development of the planet. Architecture in this sense can be experienced in a solution but it is not the solution per se. The solution might be a house, an integrated value chain, a municipal bond, or a CSIF. Great architecture ensures they work. Great architecture ensures they have the capacity to accommodate and adapt to unforeseen situations. *Great architecture is the logic* that renders solutions simultaneously timeless and of place. To reveal this architecture requires a deliberative design approach, which aligns people, opportunity, capital, place, values, and resources. The Deliberative Design Framework (DDF) comprises three core stages: outreach and alignment, implementation tactics and facility, and stewardship of implementation. At its most fundamental, the DDF contests command and control power structures, which have failed to translate sound universal policy and program thinking into local investment opportunities. Instead, it promotes a distributed model of engagement allowing for a structured approach to aligning many voices while the deliberative component provides for these voices to be heard. To this end it combines the agency of people and organizations to innovate, lead and accelerates systemic change. Part of this also involves the reframing of 'assets' whether material place-based, human, or abstracted assets such as culture that are seen as critical to building a sustainable development response. Ultimately, the DDF is grounded in a *politics about change*, and therefore the notion that deep growth and progress is about transformation and about managing the intersection between being and becoming. Without this understanding deep growth and progress is not only difficult but will fail to be sustainable.

Where do cross-sector implementation facilities (CSIF) work best? CSIF can play a critical role in localizing the global financial system and giving it a material presence by pursuing aggregated place-based impact. CSIF implement and sustain change as opposed to simply delivering technical outputs. They can play a unique role in the structural and cultural change of the financial system by connecting various scales of public, private, and civil sector interests to 'place' through a process of vertical integration. Addressing the imbalance between human and planetary systems is not a cosmetic exercise and cannot be fixed without addressing the underlying cultural and political systems that led to the imbalance in the first place. Creating sustainable cultural and in turn structural change requires new intersectional-organizational forms such as CSIF. The value of CSIF is that they can be established with contemporary forward-looking corporate values and agenda by partner-organizations, which are themselves transitioning culturally but require more immediate, nimble, and agile structures with which to engage the new value systems underpinning finance.

FLOW AND POVERTY

"If anyone owe a debt for a loan, and a storm prostrates the grain, or the harvest fail, or the grain does not grow for lack of water; in that year he need not give his creditor any grain, he washes his debt-tablet in water and pays no rent for this year." So wrote the Code of Hammurabi, a Babylonian legal text composed between 1755–1750 BC, which is one of the world's earlier known legal codes.[66] The Code of Hammurabi relieved a person in poverty from debt obligations. The question we now turn our attention to is how today's modern financial system can be structured in ways which recognise the linkages between finance and poverty.

The concept that it is expensive to be poor has been captured in literature including Robert Tressell's *The Ragged-Trousered Philanthropists.*[67] David Caplovitz's 1967 book *The Poor Pay More* considered how instalment plans lead to lower-income households paying more for televisions and kitchen appliances.[68] The concept of poverty premium was first outlined in a 2002 Harvard Business Review (HBR) article by C.K. Prahalad and Allen Hammond that described the benefits multinationals could gain by serving poor consumers in emerging markets. The UK's Social Market Foundation defines the "poverty premium" as "the extra cost that households on low incomes incur when purchasing the same essential goods and services as households on higher incomes".[69]

One of the impacts of investors accumulating more and more capital in a small number of deep capital pools means that the information that investors rely on to make decisions comes out of those same deep pools. Because financial system participants are not investing and financing places with entrenched poverty, they also have a lack of information. As a result, financial systems are not tuning into social volatility and upheaval, such as the mass movements of people, and a myriad of environmental threats, which is happening on a day-to-day basis in parts of the world. It is often said that you cannot manage what you cannot measure. Certainly, financial system participants cannot improve practices in areas where they are not involved. This is incidentally the same argument that is made in respect to an investor divesting from an oil company. Once an investor divests it is argued that they have no influence on that company. The same applies to areas where the global financial system is not actively investing. Without investment at real scale there is limited influence to improve practices. How do we get real finance to flow to the communities and the entrepreneurs who need finance? One case study is the eleven countries that make up the Sahel region. It is estimated that by 2050, the close to 200 million people living there in 2021 will rise to 500 million people. 75 percent of the population is under twenty-one years old. How do we optimize the opportunities provided by the demographic bounce coming to the Sahel? How do we improve agricultural value chains? How do we defend against desertification? This challenge will take a complete reimagining of private finance and private markets. Get the Sahel right and you can achieve the same anywhere on the planet. If financial system participants are genuinely serious about contributing to delivering the SDGs, then there is a need to get hands and feet dirty and support the development of the flow of finance for all.

On the positive side, disruption is now occurring that is resulting to the flow of finance to last mile communities. Out of many potential examples, one generic case based on real life entrepreneurial example in the rapidly evolving data-driven, digitally smart, disruptive pay-as-you-go (PayGo) sector in Africa, is distributed infrastructure that is being delivered to last mile communities. One Kenyan start up, MWEZI LTD, has accumulated 252,000 agricultural out-grower clients for clean energy solutions, productive agritech and is now exploring e-mobility as well as a range of kick start technologies for community entrepreneurs. Evolving from a shop established in a re-fitted shipping container, MWEZI is now a last mile distributor of solar products and services and is evolving into an asset-backed supplier of affordable credit with the profile of a micro-financial institution. MWEZI's mission is to provide clean energy, health, wealth, and education solutions for target peri-urban and rural African communities in a sustainable and scalable way using market-based solutions. MWEZI products and services are fashioned to improve the environmental impact of client communities. Established in March 2013, MWEZI now generates USD 70,000 of sales per month from its seventeen locations in Kenya. Founder Mike Sherry, who has been working on clean energy issues in East Africa since 2006, had observed that a lot of distributors were importing solar products from China but were not really investing in the infrastructure on the ground to support sales and after sales service. "They were essentially selling it out of the back of a van. And for me that was problematic," explained Sherry. "The people who needed the solar most also needed technical assistance for installing the product and they also needed after sales support like anyone who buys an electronic product. And it just felt to me that was a missed opportunity and it was damaging the market at the time". MWEZI set out to establish a branch network embedded in six initial target pilot communities that would create sustainable livelihoods and deepen local capabilities to run the nascent sales points and workshops. Sherry added: "What we didn't want to be is a solar company, we wanted to be a last mile distributor and we started investing in systems quite heavily. Significant investment in integrated technologies is the key to scale for MWEZI," Sherry explained. "All our sales team and support staff carry smart phones. From that smart phone, they can sell products on credit using an app. We have decided that our value is to be a last mile distributor, retailer and after sales service provider, not a manufacturer." A year into the business, MWEZI established operations in Kenya in March 2014 with branches around Lake Victoria, as well as a sales hub that is an office and training centre in Nairobi. Primarily, the company sells pay-as-you-go (PAYG) solar systems that have embedded technology that allows MWEZI to control remotely when the system works, and when it does not work. Sherry continues: “Basically when a customer has money to pay us, the system generates a code, by SMS, the customer inputs that code into the product and that unlocks it for a period depending on how much they pay. They can pay for the whole product if they wish, and therefore it unlocks, and they can use it whenever they wish. If they pay a deposit, say 20 percent, they get an appropriate amount of light or power. They get a reminder when the next payment is due. When they make the next payment, the system unlocks for another period”. MWEZI’s model allows the organization to give credit to people whilst creating an incentive to pay regularly. Sherry explained that the MWEZI system is fully automated at the point of sale and distribution. There is a chip set embedded into each product, which interacts with MWEZI software and the customer’s mobile money account. A critical issue in MWEZI’s early years has been funding the gap between the company paying for the products with cash and the customers paying for the product over time. “Larger products may take nine to ten months to pay. So, there is quite a large gap of a year from acquiring the product and the customer ultimately paying for it and owning it. That has been our critical business struggle,” Sherry added. However, the British entrepreneur sees a positive convergence of developments that will allow the business to grow, scale and replicate in other regions of the country as well as on a Pan African basis in time. “The combination of mobile phone and digital technologies, the integration of the PAYG chips in each product, and our proprietary system design after four years of experience and adjustment means we know our portfolio at risk at the end of each day.” Sherry argues that “Building accurate management information systems and knowing our customer base means that through reliable data we have options to secure backing, whether debt or equity, to grow and scale the business”. According to Sherry, MWEZI now has the potential to open an almost unlimited number of branches across Africa and, as a result, is talking to potential partners in Senegal and South Africa. MWEZI is focusing on introducing a whole range of productive solar products that are PAYG. It has introduced a PAYG solar lamp specifically designed for night fishing that gives vessels on Lake

Victoria twice the yield for half the cost. Another example of the flexibility of these products means that in addition to providing household solar, they can be used for micro-irrigation, which gives farmers twice the yield for half the water. As a last mile retailer MWEZI can introduce new products across the clean energy, health, wealth, and education spectrum as demand manifests itself from within the existing customer base. For example, reusable sanitary towels are being trialled following feedback from sales agents. "Our team are mostly women and they have seen the real demand as they go directly into customer and prospective customer households." MWEZI has a customer care centre and the team there make out-bound calls to new and, when needed, existing customers. "What we found is that people sometimes don't pay because it is a little bit complicated at first," explained Sherry. "If you have never seen a PAYG product before, it is a bit like buying your Ikea cupboard where it looks straight forward until you have a bit left over at the end. It takes a bit of familiarization. So, we have out-bound calls within twenty-four hours to those who purchase MWEZI products. We explain how PAYG works to make sure customers are familiar with the system. Accountability and customer service is as much what differentiates MWEZI as does the proprietary wiring of our digital systems." A significant impediment for businesses operating in Kenya is the cost of credit. According to Mike Sherry, mortgage interest rates in Kenya can be up to 28 percent. "What the banks ask of me, are a personal guarantee and they want to charge me 18 percent on a factoring arrangement even though it is secure. It is prohibitively expensive for everybody and that's why we are working with the fintech community to drive new solutions," concluded Sherry.

Despite a proven, replicable, and scalable model, based on world class execution and, critically listening to the needs of local communities rather than imposing technology solutions, it has MWEZI close to full eight years to secure meaningful backing from a well referenced financial institution. The battle to secure backing continually ran into the same obstacles—too small, data not good enough, and, beyond all, a cultural wall that dismisses so many promising African start-ups. One example is a Board member of a major global bank was told the story of the last mile distributor during an annual investor dinner at the World Economic Forum in Davos, Switzerland. "That's amazing and exactly what we need to back going forward. I'll put you in touch with our local people and we'll have a proper look as we are very keen on reaching the unbanked in the last mile," she confirmed. Her message was duly passed down the line until it arrived at the local branch serving the business region. Despite a clear "take a look" from the Board, the ultimate answer for any form of financing came back as an interest rate of 38 percent and the deeds to the founder's property. Similar examples became an almost Monty Python parade of how mainstream finance sees so-many promising African SMEs as "not worth bothering with" other than on punitive terms. The business is now deep in conversations with institutional, although deeply entrepreneurial, capital in Brazil and South Africa to embed a successful Kenyan last mile model there. After some near-death experiences in 2020 due to COVID-19 and questionable antics from financial backers, MWEZI by mid-2021 had secured loans and working capital backing from three prestigious funds, included blended approaches, to continue its for-profit journey to empower last mile communities, and then replicate and scale what is a smart, digital, data driven, financially disciplined, start-up. What cannot be disputed is that fifty-five thousand farming and fishing families have benefited from a for-profit form of purposeful capitalism totally aligned with the SDGs and ESG. This illustrative business example elucidates the broader point that there is no real, widespread private market infrastructure to connect institutional funds at scale to back and foster entrepreneurial endeavours, through equity, debt, mezzanine, hybrid and blended pools of capital and finance, with the potential for impact at scale for the last mile. Development Finance Institutions (DFI), both national, regional, and multilateral, will argue that this is their role, but the reality has often boiled down to a focus on larger ticket deals and other than 'show projects' they are often too disconnected from many last mile entrepreneurs. Another area is responsible investment. There has been a significant uptake of responsible investment by institutional investors, however this has yet to be accompanied by the resourcing of collaborative initiatives that support the examination of gaps in markets, particularly in less developed countries (LDC). The fast, agile, risk embracing private capital is so often missing from the equation, or limited to the pockets of the truly converted, as there is no market infrastructure to allow risk management and mitigation, and smooth transfer of assets between a well-established last mile investor class. Models like the Tony Elumelu Foundation in Nigeria, backing more than ten thousand entrepreneurs across Africa, are filling the gap many mainstream institutions and initiatives claim to have a "real interest in" but studiously avoid. The reality is that the SDGs cannot be delivered unless there is a flow of finance to all. The 2 billion people at the base of the pyramid in the last mile are the communities left furthest behind and who will experience the impacts of systemic risks such as climate change and inequality more directly than anyone else. The capacity and capability to mobilize private capital in any form to those entrepreneurs, businesses, or projects through main-stream channels is unbelievably difficult.

One opportunity may be to re-examine mutuals and cooperatives. In times past, those with the least resources found ways to support each other. The development of mutuals, cooperatives, friendly societies and building societies are in fact the genesis of the modern fiduciary financial institution. Today it is arguable that financial systems consist of two major players – governments and the private sector. For many reasons mutuals have become constrained in their ability to participate in modern financial systems. Rebuilding the missing middle is core to flow finance for all. Mutuals are organizations that are owned and run for the benefit of members. Mutuals do not have to pay dividends and can use profits to deliver member benefits. The links between the development of mutuals and mutualism and our modern financial system deserve deeper study. Mutualism did not invent finance, but some of the key innovations that have profoundly changed lives and have become the core to today's modern financial system came from mutuals. The first insurance companies were in fact fire brigades where an individual would place a "fire mark" on the door of their house so that the insurance company could know whether to help put a fire out. The first building societies in the United Kingdom were established around 1775 out of taverns and coffee houses. The world's first building society, Ketley's Building Society[70], was founded by Richard Ketley who was the landlord at the Golden Cross Inn in Birmingham, England, in 1775. Members (otherwise known as drinkers at the pub) would pool resources and draw lots to select which of the members would have land purchased and a house constructed. Affordable life insurance products became available in the nineteenth century dominated by Scottish based institutions such as Scottish Mutual, Scottish Equitable and Standard Life. The evocatively named Scottish Widows was set up in 1815 to take care of women and children who lost their fathers, brothers, and husbands in the Napoleonic Wars, taking its name after the people it was founded to care for. Members of friendly societies such as the Independent Order of Odd Fellows (IOOF) in Australia would make a payment at local lodge meetings. In the event of injury, worker's families would be provided with income for household necessities therefore preventing destitution. Cooperatives are another form of mutual. The Rochdale Pioneers were established in 1844 by a group of twenty-eight workers in cotton mills in the town of Rochdale, Lancashire, pooling their scarce resources and working together they could access basic goods at a lower price. Initially, there were only four items for sale: flour, oatmeal, sugar, and butter. Today it is estimated that there are around 3 million mutuals worldwide. The Top 300 cooperatives and mutuals have a reported total turnover of over USD 2,146 billion, yet mutuals have largely been squeezed out of modern financial markets. The irony is that pension funds who are themselves organizations established for the mutual benefit of members, contribute to the marginalization of mutuals through asset allocation strategies, which prioritize investments in share equity and corporate and government bonds. The impact is that mutuals have found it difficult to raise capital to meet new needs, which has entrenched the loss of missing middle of finance.

Another identified area of need are refugees. Today the number of people who have been displaced from their homes is comparable to the end of World War II. The scope of recent humanitarian crises has led to a shift in thinking on who is responsible for supporting refugees. The sheer numbers of displaced people mean that there is an urgent need to share responsibility. This chapter considers the role that the private sector, and specifically the financial system can play in supporting refugees. The successful example of income contingent loan (ICL) schemes in higher education is considered as a template for the development of refugee income contingent loan schemes. According to United Nations High Commissioner for Refugees (UNHCR), as at the end of 2019 there were 20.2 million refugees and 43.5 million internally displaced people across the globe.[71] The numbers of displaced people today is comparable to the end of the World War II (WWII) when it is estimated that around 60 million Europeans were refugees.[72] In the aftermath of WWII, the United Nations High Commissioner for Refugees (UNHCR) was established on December 14, 1950, with a mandate to protect and support refugees at the request of a government or the United Nations. The role of UNHCR includes assisting in providing durable solutions, such as return or resettlement. In the same period that UNHCR was established, the United Nations General Assembly agreed to the UN Convention on the Status of Refugees,[73] establishing rights for the treatment of refugees including the right to primary education, right to work and the provision of travel documents. Following the Syrian refugee crisis that resulted from the Syrian Civil War, the United Nations General Assembly unanimously adopted on September 19, 2016, the New York Declaration for Refugees and Migrants. In adopting the New York Declaration, nations agreed that protecting refugees and supporting the countries that shelter refugees is a shared international responsibility that must be borne more equitably and predictably. Nations agreed upon the core elements of a Comprehensive Refugee Response Framework including working towards the adoption of a global compact on refugees and a global compact for safe, orderly, and regular migration. The New York Declaration paved the way for the establishment of the Global Compact on Refugees.[74] Agreed to by the United Nations General Assembly on December 17, 2018, the Compact is a framework for more predictable and equitable responsibility-sharing, providing a blueprint for governments, international organizations, and other stakeholders to ensure that host communities get the support they need and that refugees can lead productive lives. The Compact's four key objectives are to ease the pressures on host countries, enhance refugee self-reliance, expand access to third-country solutions and support conditions in countries of origin for return in safety and dignity. The Global Compact for Refugees is the conduit through which stakeholders can publicly indicate their commitment to support refugees.[75] Financial institutions that have made pledges in support of the Global Compact for Refugees include la Caixa Banking Foundation, 17 Asset Management, Bank of Ireland, Bennelong Foundation and Funds Management, Bloomberg, BNP Paribas, Developing World Markets Asset Management, Grameen Credit Agricole Foundation, ING Bank, KIMS Microfinance Kaah, Mastercard and Rabobank.[76] One of the implications of recent refugee crises has been to broaden responsibility or action to include a wide group of stakeholders. Different groups have actively taken on this responsibility. An example is the International Forum on Local Solutions to Migration and Displacement that was held on November 26, 2019, and November 27, 2019, in the city of Gaziantep, which currently hosted Syrian refugees. The forum, co-hosted by the Gaziantep Metropolitan Municipality (GMM) and the United Nations Development Programme (UNDP), brought together mayors from municipalities around the world. The resulting Gaziantep Declaration highlighted "the importance of cities being at the centre of global efforts to secure safe, inclusive and sustainable living environments" and the "importance of working with international donors and other sources of finance to support municipalities with resources to create innovative approaches to delivery of better services for refugee and migrant communities".[77] The sharing of responsibility for refugees, supported through the United Nations Global Compact for Refugees, provides the platform to consider the role of finance, and the role of the finance sector, in supporting refugees. One of the major challenges that refugees face once in situ in a host country is participating in the local economy. Whilst the UN Convention on the Status of Refugees makes clear that refugees have a right to work, there are many challenges that must be overcome to access employment. One impediment to being able to participate in employment is the lack of financial resources. One of the discussion points at the International Forum on Local Solutions to Migration and Displacement was the observation that in recent crises there were three waves of refugees. The first wave of refugees consists of independently wealthy people who have the capacity to make active choices, the second wave consists of middle-class individuals whose income is attached to their employment but who have some economic means whilst the third wave of refugees are those that literally flee with nothing but the shirts on their backs.[78] It is second and third waves that need to be the focus of financial systems. Refugees commonly lack financial resources to establish themselves. In some cases, the need is as basic as the inability to access clothing that is culturally appropriate. Whilst many governments have refugee settlement programs, the reality is that many refugees start lives in host countries without the basics that enable participation in work. This can include the inability to access a car, tools of trade or a computer. The lack of financial resources is exacerbated by the inability to access finance from financial institutions. Banks offer credit to individuals based on risk. The interest rate offered by a bank reflects its rating of risk. Individuals that are regarded as having low credit risk, or who can secure credit against assets, are able to access the lowest interest rates. Individuals that are regarded as having high credit risk pay the most to access credit. There is a cruel irony that in a world where there is currently USD 18 trillion of bonds with negative yields[79] that the poorest individuals in society may only be able to access credit at interest rates of 200 percent.[80]

Whilst refugees may start with nothing, evidence suggests that they make valuable contributions to the countries in which they reside. Research by Kalena E. Cortes[81] provides evidence that refugee immigrants have higher rates of human capital accumulation than economic migrants.

Using 1980/1990 Integrated Public Use Samples of the US Census, Cortes's research examined labor market outcomes of immigrants who arrived in the US from 1975 to 1980. Refugees in 1980 earned 6 percent less and worked 14 percent fewer hours than economic immigrants. By 1990 however the labor market outcomes of refugee immigrants surpassed those of economic immigrants. In 1990, refugees from the 1975-1980 arrival cohort earned 20 percent more, worked 4 percent more hours, and improved their English skills by 11 percent relative to economic immigrants. Cortes argues that because refugees lack the option of emigration back to their homeland, they may be more inclined to invest in country-specific human capital in the form of improving language skills, becoming naturalized citizens, and enrolling in the host nation's educational system. Whilst Cortes research was for a specific period, the proposition that refugees have strong incentives to invest in human capital accumulation has implications for participation in a domestic financial system. It can be argued that the situation that refugees find themselves in when they arrive in a host country is comparable to the situation of a student facing tuition fees to access higher education. In this regard, the experience of the development of income contingent loans (ICL), which has provided a solution to address a market failure for students, is relevant to refugees. The question is whether lessons from higher education ICL schemes can be applied to refugees. An argument is that Refugee ICL schemes could provide a pathway for refugees to access formal financial systems rather than relying on access to finance to meet needs through higher forms of credit such as pay day loans. The challenge facing a prospective lender considering a loan to a student borrower is that the lack of collateral, and the risk that the future value of an individual's human capital could turn out to be low, act as a disincentive for the financial system to provide credit.[82] Examining the role of government in education in 1955, Milton Friedman[83] argued that underinvestment in human capital reflected an imperfection in the capital market. He stated, "investment in human beings cannot be financed on the same terms or with the same ease as investment in physical capital. It is easy to see why there would be such a difference.

If a fixed money loan is made to finance investment in physical capital, the lender can get some security for his loan in the form of a mortgage or residual claim to the physical asset itself, and he can count on realizing at least part of his investment in case of necessity by selling the physical asset. If he makes a comparable loan to increase the earning power of a human being, he clearly cannot get any comparable security; in a non-slave state, the individual embodying the investment cannot be bought and sold". Friedman argued that because investing in education delivered benefits not only to an individual but to society, there was a "neighbourhood effect". Friedman proposed that individuals should not be prevented by market imperfections from making the investment when they are willing to bear the costs. He proposed that, "A governmental body could offer to finance or help finance the training of any individual who could meet minimum quality standards by making available not more than a limited sum per year for not more than a specified number of years, provided it was spent on securing training at a recognized institution. The individual would agree in return to pay to the government in each future year x per cent of his earnings in excess of y dollars for each USD 1,000 that he gets in this way. This payment could easily be combined with payment of income tax and so involve a minimum of additional administrative expense." Friedman's idea of a government income contingent loan scheme for higher education was implemented thirty years later when the Australian Government introduced the Higher Education Contribution Scheme (HECS) in 1989. Eight other countries have since adopted similar student loan schemes. The success of HECS has subsequently led to discussion[84] on how income contingent loans (ICL) can be used for other purposes including the payment of fines for low level criminal activity, social investment community projects, climate change adaptation policies and small business loans.[85]

Refugee Income Contingent Loan Scheme could either be developed by governments or the private sector. The argument in favour of governments establishing Refugee Income Contingent Loan Schemes is that because repayment of an income contingent loan depends on knowing the income of a borrower, internal revenue services are in a strong position to manage schemes because they have the legal jurisdiction to know a citizen's income and the apparatus to collect efficiently.[86] Governments also have the capacity to efficiently provide education programs that are a necessary accompaniment to any form of credit. The ability to leverage the lessons from the experience of countries such as Australia that have implemented and managed income contingent loans schemes for higher education also provides a clear comparative advantage to the private sector in implementing and managing an income contingent loan scheme for refugees. The challenge that governments may face in introducing a scheme is to overcome local resistance. Resistance may manifest itself in two ways. Firstly, policy makers may be reluctant to provide benefits to a group where they do not provide similar benefits to their own community. Secondly, policy makers may be concerned that the introduction of an income contingent loan scheme may, despite the clear definition of refugees under the UN Refugee Convention, act to pull demand for economic migrants to come to a country. An example of the focus to deter economic migration is the EU and Italy's funding of the Libyan Coast Guard from 2017.[87] The first issue is in some ways easier to deal with than the second issue. Economists have argued that in the light of COVID-19 that it makes sense to provide income and revenue contingent loans to individuals and small businesses alike.[88] There is the potential for governments to develop schemes that specifically address crises situations. Examples of the ways in which income contingent loan schemes could be widened to achieve broader community support would be to enable individuals fleeing domestic violence, or individuals dealing with the impact of catastrophic floods, fires, and droughts to access an income contingent loan scheme. Australia provides a recent case study of the economic and social impact of catastrophic weather events. The summer fires of 2019-20 resulted in the loss of 33 lives, with 3,094 houses lost and 38,416 insurance claims.[89] The need for financial mechanisms to address catastrophes has been in the past dealt with in an ad-hoc manner. An ICL scheme linked to social services could be developed to provide a permanent capacity for governments to financially support individual through crisis events. If this was the case, refugees could be able to access government ICL schemes. One issue where governments have a clear comparative advantage in providing finance is the cost of credit. As discussed earlier in the book there is currently USD 18 trillion of bonds that are earning negative yields. Much of this debt is provided in the form of sovereign bonds to nations. The cost of credit for governments has never been cheaper.

The challenge that the financial sector has in establishing a Refugee Income Contingent Loan Scheme are regulatory frameworks that require financial institution to account for the value of assets. For the banking sector, the Basel Committee on Banking Supervision's Basel III framework requires banks, and their domestic financial sector regulators, to establish "prudent valuation for positions that are accounted for at fair value, whether they are in the trading book or in the banking book ... Banks must establish and maintain adequate systems and controls sufficient to give management and supervisors the confidence that their valuation estimates are prudent and reliable".[90] There may not be restrictions for a bank to establish a Refugee ICL. It may come down to their risk appetite. The challenge with income contingent loan schemes in general is the difficulty in assessing the "fair value" of the asset, in this case a loan. This does not mean that it is impossible for the financial sector to implement and manage an income contingent loan scheme. But to do so is likely to require some sort of regulatory approval. One way to do this is for regulators to provide capital relief for banks to invest in a structure that manages income contingent loans. A precedent for this in Australia is the Australian Prudential Regulatory Authority's adjustment of its capital framework, which enabled Australian banks to invest in the Australian Business Growth Fund (ABGF) to provide longer term equity funding to small and medium-sized enterprises (SMEs).[91] Whilst regulatory frameworks make it difficult, but not impossible, for banks to provide ICLs to any customers, let alone refugees, technology change is assisting the financial system to manage one of the critical components of an ICL; the need to be able to identify the income of an individual. Due to the growth of digital payments, banks are in a stronger position to be able to assess income than they would have been historically. Accenture forecasts nearly 420 billion transactions worth USD 7 trillion are expected to shift from cash to cards and digital payments by 2023 – and increase to USD 48 trillion by 2030.[92] A strong argument for the involvement of financial system participants in a refugee ICL is the opportunity to link to consumer credit scores. A consumer credit score is designed to measure the risk of default of a consumer by taking into consideration a person's financial history. Credit scores are used by financial institutions as part of decision-making process for new loans. Whilst credit scoring systems will differ according to the jurisdiction, a key criterion that determines an individual's credit score is their payment history. In this regard, there is the potential that successfully paying off a refugee ICL can provide an individual with a positive credit score that can assist them to access future loans from financial institutions.

The challenge with the first two identified pathways is the danger that, despite the merits of establishing an ICL scheme for refugees, because of the obstacles to establishing a scheme the status quo continues to exist. The development of a partnership between financial system participants, government and stakeholders including the philanthropic community may provide an alternative pathway. Two different stakeholder partnerships are briefly discussed. The first pathway is to develop a pilot at a national level that demonstrates the workability of a refugee ICL scheme. The second pathway is to establish an international partnership using existing international organizations to drive the development of a universal scheme. Each pathway is briefly considered. Establishing a pilot ICL refugee scheme provides a mechanism for partners to iteratively build practices. A pilot scheme needs to establish transparency to enable lessons to be applied in other jurisdictions to implement their own schemes. Ideally, a domestic pilot would involve financial system participants, government, regulators, and philanthropic community. Each participant has specific roles to play. Financial system participants can provide a loan platform and capital. Government can provide education program and regulatory support whilst philanthropic and not-for-profit community can provide capital and access to refugee support groups. A key consideration is the structure of a stakeholder partnership. Trust structures are commonly established as a mechanism for municipal bonds and could provide a workable structure for a loan scheme. The cost of credit could be addressed through government support. Government could either borrow on behalf of the trust or could act as a credit guarantor. The result is that there is the potential that at the current rates of borrowing in capital markets that funds could be provided to the trust at close to zero interest rates. Five United Nations bodies are identified that could jointly convene a working group that could facilitate international Refugee ICL stakeholder partnership: United Nations Environment Programme Finance Initiative (UNEP FI), United Nations High Commissioner for Refugees (UNHCR), United Nations Development Programme (UNDP), United Nations Conference for Trade and Development (UNCTAD), and United Nations Global Compact. Precedent for UN bodies convening to establish an initiative that crosses over responsibilities is the Sustainable Stock Exchanges Initiative where UNCTAD, UN Global Compact, UNEP FI, and the Principles for Responsible Investment (PRI) are the founding partners. A Sustainable Finance for Refugees Initiative (SFRI) is proposed as a means through which separate UN bodies can work together. Regardless of the pathway to develop Refugee ICLs, there are several design issues that a scheme needs to consider.

Use of finance: There is the potential for a scheme to determine how prescriptive the proceeds from finance should be. Higher education ICLs such as HECS in Australia have traditionally not sought to determine what an individual should study on the basis that they are in the best position to determine what they are interested in and have capability to succeed at. A similar principle could be adopted for a Refugee ICL, that is, individuals are in the best position to determine what it is that they need.

Amount of finance: The amount of finance, and the potential for an individual to have a second ICL on successful repayment of an initial ICL can be considered in design.

Linkage to credit scores: Successful repayment of an ICL has the potential to be linked to credit scoring systems that exist in each jurisdiction.

Rate of interest: The nature of a broadly based ICL scheme is that there will be a portion of borrowers who do not pay back their original loans. Higher education ICL schemes have been built around this expectation. The design of a scheme can either seek to cover its costs (in which case it will need a positive interest rate to cover administration cost and factor in the number of loans that may not be repaid). Alternatively, loans can be subsidized by government or philanthropic community.

Refugees in many countries including the United States, Germany, United Kingdom and Australia have made major economic and social contributions to their host nations. The history of the economic contribution of refugees goes back hundreds of years. An example are the Huguenots who fled religious prosecution in France in the 1620s, with between 40,000 and 50,000 refugees accepting Charles II offer of sanctuary.[93] The town of Spitalfields became a destination for Huguenot weavers supporting the development of fashions in England at the time.[94] It falls to our generation of financial system participants to design and implement the structures that will enable people to access affordable credit. In a world where trillions of dollars do not earn a positive rate of interest, it is unacceptable that interest rates as high as 200 percent can be charged to vulnerable communities. A pathway forward is to establish Income Contingent Loans for Refugees. We propose that actions occur at both a national and local level as well as at an international level through the establishment of a Sustainable Finance for Refugees Initiative.

The key purpose of this chapter has been to discuss ways in which financial systems can support individuals and communities that are in poverty. Whether learning from the past through the history of mutuals and cooperatives, through to understanding the impediments facing innovative entrepreneurship in Africa or the opportunity through policy nudges to open access to finance for refugees, we demonstrate ways in which financial systems can support addressing poverty.

FLOW TO INFRASTRUCTURE

The urgent need for new infrastructure investment coupled with the financial impacts of the COVID-19 crisis is coinciding with the rapid disruption of infrastructure through new technology. The impact of this disruption is so profound that, for the first time in history, it is possible to articulate an ambition of universal infrastructure coverage.[95]

Long after the COVID-19 virus has dissipated, its impacts on the global economy and society will still be felt. One impact, beyond the health impacts, is that the world will emerge from the pandemic more indebted. According to the Institute of International Finance, the global debt burden is set to rise dramatically in 2020, having already risen by over USD 10 trillion in 2019. High levels of debt will have several long-term implications for governments. As developing economies examine the tools at their disposal to rebuild while simultaneously seeking to ensure that they are prepared for future risks—including most particularly climate change—more than ever, there will be a need for private sector investment in infrastructure. The question is: How can private infrastructure investment be increased at scale post-pandemic?

There is broad agreement that there is a need for more infrastructure investment to address the challenges of climate change. At the 2018 Buenos Aires G20 summit, the Organisation for Economic Co-operation and Development (OECD), UN Environment, and the World Bank released a report, *Financing Climate Futures: Rethinking Infrastructure*, that argued that investing in infrastructure is not only vital to the sustainability of the planet, but it also has the capacity to drive economic growth. Introducing the report Gabriela Ramos, OECD Chief of Staff and G20 Sherpa, said, "We are losing time though—if we want to deliver, we need to move much faster and achieve a systemic shift of trillions of dollars in green investment." Infrastructure is a critical component to delivering the Sustainable Development Goals (SDGs). The term universal infrastructure coverage[96] (UIC) references the United Nations General Assembly resolution from December 12, 2012, that urges countries to accelerate progress toward universal health coverage (UHC)—the idea that everyone, everywhere should have access to quality, affordable health care—an essential priority for international development. According to the World Health Organization, UHC means that all people have access to the health services they need, when and where they need them, without financial hardship. Despite the acknowledged importance of infrastructure, we have yet to translate the urgent need to invest in infrastructure into a common language and a common ambition. Infrastructure is a critical component to delivering the SDGs. If we are unable to provide universal infrastructure coverage for communities across the globe, then the task of delivering the SDGs and addressing climate change becomes exponentially more challenging. Establishing an ambition for universal infrastructure coverage recognizes that the disruption that is occurring in infrastructure is reducing the capital cost that is required to deliver outcomes. Energy is an example. No longer are expensive investments in electricity grids the only pathway to generate energy. With the combination of solar and battery technology, micro-grids are not only feasible but preferable in many remote regions. Coupled with the provision of stand-alone, off-grid solar systems through for-profit, Pay-As-You-Go (PAYGO) last-mile distributors, the pivot to a distributed energy infrastructure offering deeper energy security in combination with the on-grid architecture becomes a powerful developmental engine for change. Infrastructure is subject to the same forces of technology disruption that have impacted established sectors, including newspapers, music, and high street retail businesses. Today we stand at a watershed moment where technology is disrupting infrastructure service delivery models. There are many examples of disruption, including across transportation, energy, and water. A range of technology innovations are being implemented that are improving the efficiency of transit systems and are less capital intensive than large-scale infrastructure projects, including on-demand ride-sharing services, e-bikes, intelligent traffic signals, smart parking, and on-demand buses. The rise of electric vehicles (EVs) is resulting in the development of EV infrastructure with the US President Biden outlining a plan to build 500,000 electric vehicle charging stations across the country. COVID-19 has led to a massive shift to working from home, which in turn has opened conversations among city planners around designing spaces to reduce the need for transit so that people can live and work in their communities. The combination of the application of smart technology, the emergence of EV infrastructure, and shifting transport patterns is changing the playing field in favour of small-scale infrastructure investments rather than mega transport projects. The rise of low-cost solar energy is changing the fundamentals of electric grid management. In 2013, California's energy system regulator, the California Independent System Operator, labelled anticipated changes to the electric grid from the uptake of large-scale solar photovoltaic (PV) generation as the "duck curve". The duck curve reflects the fact that solar energy is variable, as it is produced only when the sun is shining. As more solar comes into the grid, the net load that electricity grids need to supply from other energy sources falls. The rise of solar has implications for sources of energy such as coal-fired power stations, which are unable to easily adapt the level of energy supply. The impact of the duck curve is to influence new infrastructure investments. Instead of needing large-scale power stations, demand is shifting to adaptable energy sources, including the development of battery storage systems. Responding to shifting energy supply and demand patterns, some energy participants, such as New Zealand's Mercury and Australia's AGL, are transforming their business models. Future energy businesses will not only be in the businesses of supplying energy. Mercury has developed an EV subscription service aimed at opening access to EVs without up-front commitment or costs, insulating drivers from depreciation, maintenance, and insurance costs. AGL's EV subscription service charges a monthly fee in return for the installation of EV charging infrastructure at the home, insurance, and maintenance. The assumption that power needs to be delivered from one central place (coal-fired power station) to another (city) is being challenged by the growth of PAYGO systems that are delivering off-grid solar sector to 420 million users. In the MWEZI case study discussed earlier, clean energy is being supplied in Kenya via PAYGo solar systems. According to the World Bank, the off-grid solar sector is now a USD 1.75 billion annual market currently serving 420 million users. With 840 million people without access to electricity and over 1 billion people connected to unreliable grids, the development of off-grid solar enables developing countries to access affordable electricity for all their communities. The opportunity for off-grid solar has come not just from the development of solar technology but from the availability of mobile phones and bank payment systems that are opening access to PAYGO-enabled products that enable individuals to access the amount of energy needed to suit their needs and circumstances.

The importance of water and sanitation systems was recognized during the International Decade of Clean Water (1980–1991) when bringing clean water to an extra 1.2 billion people achieved huge improvements in child mortality. Despite many achievements over the last few decades, 2.4 billion people still lack access to basic sanitation services, such as toilets or latrines. More than 80 percent of wastewater resulting from human activities is still discharged into rivers or seas without any pollution removal. The growth of mega-cities is resulting in the demand for water exceeding what can be delivered by rainwater harvesting. Over 40 percent of the world's population is likely to be living in river basins that are expected to be under severe stress by 2050. This equates to roughly 3.9 billion people. Technology disruptions in the water sector include new approaches to demand management and investments to increase supply through desalinization. The development of distributed water supplies, which includes the installation of household water tanks and local treatment of bore water, is turning households into water suppliers as well as consumers. Technology is now enabling small-scale investment in water infrastructure that recognizes the scarcity of water resources. For example, smart water systems enable recycled water to be used for a variety of purposes, including flushing toilets. K-Water in South Korea, for example, is investing in establishing a smart water grid combining the existing grid with information and communication technologies. A sensor network within pipelines enables K-Water to analyse water quality, pressure, and leakage. In another example, in Denver, Colorado, recycled water from a wastewater treatment plant is supplying 30 million gallons per day to eighty customers, including the Denver Zoo. Water scarcity that will result from increased population and climate change is likely to blur the boundaries between the traditional activities of water utilities: provision of potable water and removal of wastewater. The development of opportunities to use recycled water in urban contexts is likely to become a fundamental focus for water utilities and offers the potential for households and businesses to become producers, not just consumers, of water.

The emergence of distributed infrastructure has implications for the structures that can be used to finance infrastructure. Within infrastructure circles, there is considerable discussion around the term's "project" and "asset". In *Infrastructure as an Asset Class*, Weber et al. provide clarity on the terms, stating: "Investment in infrastructure projects primarily differ from those in infrastructure assets as in the former, the investor does not necessarily become the full or partial owner of the assets in question. Rather, the investor invests in or finances the provision of the asset and in exchange is granted either the revenues generated by the project or regular payment from the principle during the course of a clearly defined project." The differentiation between "project" and "asset" is important when it comes to the emergence of distributed infrastructure systems. In the case of distributed infrastructure, a project structure makes little sense. The nature of distributed infrastructure is that the asset, which could include thousands of portable solar systems, is able to be physically owned. Because distributed infrastructure assets can be owned, a traditional company structure, rather than a project structure, is the ideal means to finance the asset. Establishing infrastructure as a business rather than as a project provides an ideal structure that enables adaptation in the face of uncertainty. For developing countries, developing infrastructure through a traditional business structure has several benefits. A challenge with infrastructure projects is how to capture the spillover benefits that result from financing, building, and operating an individual project. Currently, with large-scale infrastructure projects, individual project managers take knowledge away from a project, which is utilized in the next project that is delivered. Establishing a business offers the opportunity to retain skills that can be used to build long-term and sustainable regional capabilities. The benefit of building an infrastructure business is that once the governance, capital structure, and management are in place, the business has the capacity to expand, whereas a project structure is limited to the single project that is being delivered. Using a traditional company structure enables policymakers to consider local stock exchanges as a mechanism to raise finance. Listing an infrastructure business on a local stock exchange aligns with the large pools of institutional capital. Approximately USD 70 trillion in assets is managed by institutional investors, including pension funds, insurers, and sovereign wealth funds. Pension funds alone have an estimated USD 20 trillion—21 trillion in assets, with the top three hundred pension funds in the world managing around USD 15.7 trillion. Equity markets are where institutional investors already allocate the bulk of their capital. The investment models and systems of asset owners have been built around utilizing equity markets as the principal mechanism to allocate capital. Investing in infrastructure businesses through stock exchanges is not new. There are two major pools of institutional infrastructure equity investment: Listed equity and unlisted private equity. According to the Global Listed Infrastructure Organization (GLIO), the market capitalization of listed infrastructure is around USD 2.5 trillion. By contrast, according to infrastructure industry analyst Preqin, as of June 2019, there is USD 582 billion in private unlisted infrastructure assets. Listing an infrastructure business on a local stock exchange has the potential to support the development of that financial market. If a local stock exchange can attract institutional investors to invest in infrastructure businesses, then there is the potential that investors expand their horizon to investing in other stocks. In this way, investing in an infrastructure business on a local stock exchange may provide a pathway for long-term-focused institutional investors to support the expansion of developing-country stock exchanges. A local infrastructure business also benefits from increased local market activity in the form of enhanced liquidity, which addresses one of the major impediments that institutional investors experience when investing in less-developed country stock exchanges. Market liquidity, which is defined as the extent to which an individual or firm can quickly purchase or sell an asset without causing a drastic change in the asset's price, is critical for institutional investors who need to rebalance portfolios to meet the demands of their clients, including pension funds. The World Federation of Exchanges recognizes that liquidity is an impediment to investment in many developing market stock exchanges with many emerging markets suffering from significantly low levels of trading venue liquidity, effectively placing a constraint on economic and market development. It is also an advantage for policymakers that the market architecture for stock exchanges already exists. The World Federation of Exchanges (WFE) has found that markets with higher corporate governance standards attract more investment. Developing-country stock exchanges have been raising their corporate governance standards to attract institutional investment. An example is the Nigerian Stock Exchange, which launched a comprehensive Corporate Governance Rating System in November 2014 that then linked to new listings. Borsa Istanbul reformed its corporate governance requirements for companies in January 2014 with a focus on leadership, board composition, auditing, and disclosure. Developing-economy stock exchanges have also been focusing efforts on building environmental, social, and governance (ESG) criteria and sustainability capabilities with Borsa Istanbul launching its BIST Sustainability

Index to benchmark company performance on ESG metrics. Investing in partnerships with institutional investors offers an alternative for governments to contractual arrangements such as public–private partnerships (PPPs). An example of a government investing in partnership through a local stock exchange is the New Zealand Government, which holds 51 percent of Mercury NZ Ltd with the remaining shares traded on the New Zealand Stock Exchange (NZX). Investing in a partnership through a local stock exchange addresses one of the challenges of the traditional PPP model, which is the difficulty of placing an accurate value on an infrastructure development at the point of inception. If a PPP contract results in higher returns for an infrastructure investor than expected at the time of negotiation, this can create tensions among the local community and lead to pressure for government intervention. The benefit of governments and institutional investors investing together is that, when an infrastructure business delivers a better-than-expected performance, the returns are shared. Structuring infrastructure as a business that is jointly owned by governments and institutional investors enables the business to adapt. In the case of New Zealand's Mercury NZ Limited, the business has established an e-transport business that enables customers to buy e-bikes and e-scooters at a discount, as well as leasing EVs. The ability of Mercury to move into new markets that reflect the impacts of technological disruption would not have been possible under a traditional contractual structure. Establishing infrastructure as a co-owned business provides a platform that enables adaptation. With the emergence of distributed infrastructure, a shift to building infrastructure businesses requires a focus on business management. For governments wishing to ensure that an infrastructure business aligns with the long-term needs of the community, stewardship principles can provide a way of aligning the way the business is managed with the community. Stewardship is not a new concept, as it dates to ancient times where a council or regent would govern for an underage king. In modern times, renowned strategist Peter Senge took the concept of stewardship forward in 1990 with his book, *The Fifth Discipline*, which introduced the role of stewards as leaders in learning organizations. According to Senge, leaders are stewards of an organization's vision. Later, Peter Block reframed the concept of stewardship for a corporation. His concept of stewardship was to build companies with a focus on accountability without control or compliance. According to Block, "it is possible for us to decide that stewardship for the long run, for the community, for the earth, is a purpose more important than profit." Stewardship has more recently been applied to investment. The United Kingdom's Stewardship Code 2020 defines stewardship as: "The responsible allocation, management and oversight of capital to create long-term value for clients and beneficiaries leading to sustainable benefits for the economy, the environment and society." There are several tools that developing-country governments can use to embed stewardship principles into management practice including masterplans, embedding sustainability into the infrastructure business purpose and strategy and requiring high levels of public transparency. An infrastructure business should be required to submit a masterplan every three to five years that outlines the strategic plans for the asset, how this strategic plan is relevant to the needs of tomorrow's citizens, and how sustainability issues will be incorporated into management practices. The process of establishing a masterplan provides an opportunity to engage stakeholders to understand their concerns and enables new technology to be embedded into infrastructure on an ongoing basis. A masterplan also provides an opportunity to consider what an infrastructure business can achieve outside of its core activities. An example of the requirement to produce a regular masterplan comes from Australia's Airports Act 1996, which established a regulatory framework for privatized airports that aimed to support the delivery of infrastructure services and new capital investment. The act requires airports to establish a master plan that includes specifying the development objectives of the airport. Consultation with local communities is embedded into the requirements of the masterplan. In the case of Brisbane Airport's 2020 Master Plan, the opportunity to use the airport's central position and networks is being used to develop property that can provide a wide range of functional uses. Where governments are co-investors of an infrastructure business, the question is how its shareholding can be used to influence the way the infrastructure business is managed. Sustainability should be embedded into the organization's purpose and strategy because an organization's business strategy determines its resource allocation. If sustainability is not embedded into the strategy, then it will always struggle to attract the attention of the organization's executives. Government-owned assets are commonly subject to the scrutiny of parliaments, which provide an opportunity for elected officials to question all aspects of an operation. In many cases, privately owned infrastructure businesses are held in unlisted vehicles where there are no requirements to publicly report performance. A co-owned infrastructure business should provide a high level of transparency. The enterprise should publicly disclose its performance and ongoing strategy, incorporating best practice reporting and, when it has the capacity, report on climate change. Annual reports should be presented publicly with stakeholders invited to attend and direct questions to executives. An accountability regime that ensures an infrastructure business is held accountable for its actions should be in place. As well as ongoing masterplans should be created that set the direction for the future adaptability of the asset. There is a need to ensure that an infrastructure enterprise is meeting the needs of their customers daily.

Turning the current trickle of capital that is being invested in developing-country infrastructure into a mighty river comes down to recognizing that the emergence of distributed infrastructure is a game changer. It creates the possibility of universal infrastructure coverage, establishing infrastructure as a business that is co-owned by governments and institutional investors that is listed on local stock exchanges and supporting the management of infrastructure businesses through the development and implementation of stewardship principles. If we are unable to provide universal infrastructure coverage for communities across the globe, then the task of delivering the SDGs and addressing climate change becomes exponentially more challenging. Developing a new investment model that enables and facilitates universal infrastructure coverage will require new capabilities, including the development of stewardship principles that will align the management of an infrastructure business with its community. In summary, achieving the ambition of universal infrastructure coverage comes down to three simple propositions: Firstly, recognize that the emergence of distributed infrastructure is a game changer that creates the possibility of universal infrastructure coverage. Secondly, establish infrastructure as a business that is co-owned by governments and institutional investors and that is listed on local stock exchanges. Thirdly, support the management of infrastructure businesses through the development and implementation of stewardship principles.

FLOW TO MARKETS

In today's financialized economy, markets are the means through which financial systems allocate capital. Because of their importance, we need to understand their foundations, and more particularly what it takes to create new markets. The history of the development of markets demonstrates the importance of localized markets that are connected to the real economy. From the development of trade routes including the Persian Royal Road and Silk Road, to the development of market towns, markets always connected to the society that they came from. Historically, the growth of individual centres of trade such as London, Amsterdam and Venice were always accompanied by strong local markets. The challenge we identify today is that as global financial markets are becoming deeper and deeper, local markets are not benefiting from this strength but are in fact arguably becoming weaker. Once a market is established, there is a tendency for it to become self-reinforcing. Intuitively, this makes sense. If a farmer is selling apples at a wholesale market, it makes sense to go to the market where all produce can be sold quickly and efficiently. This same dynamic applies to financial markets and is one of the reasons why corporations are attracted to deep markets. The existence of a deep market attracts new participants whether it be a seller of apples in a medieval market town or a business seeking access to new equity on a stock exchange.

For markets to support the low of finance for all we need to ask two questions. Firstly, where should the leadership come from to develop markets? And secondly, once we know where the leadership comes from, how is it possible to execute a strategy to grow markets outside of the existing dominant financial markets? To answer the first question on where the leadership comes from to develop markets the first instinct is to think of institutional structures. There is a long list of institutions that play a role in international financial markets that all have a role to play in developing markets for sustainable development. But before we jump into a list of institutions and what they could do, there is a value in discussing what they should not do—and that is to focus on individual transactions. A great deal of energy is currently dedicated by international financial institutions including the World Bank, International Finance Corporation, and multilateral institutions to individual transactions. There is a broader question as to why organizations that are focused on sustainable development have been principally structured as transactional businesses. There is no doubt that individual transactions are needed to kick start activity, particularly in an environment that is coming out of conflict where institutional structures may have become corrupted or manipulated for political gains. However, there is a need for individual transactions to be accompanied by attention on developing the market ecosystem, which supports the development of future transactions. To understand the reason why individual transactions in themselves do not build effective markets an illustrative example is that of a medieval market town, simply because this creates sufficient distance from existing institutional structures to enable examining the dynamics of market building from a theoretical basis. If we go back to the example of the *Domesday Book* in 1086, England had a dominant market city where the Normans ran their operations from. The evidence remains today of the power and might of the Tower of London as a military stronghold. At that time, the *Domesday Book* records that there were sixty market towns across England. There are logical reasons why the Normans wanted to know how many market towns existed. A market town would have been seen as an indication of wealth, and therefore ability to tax. The structure of medieval towns around a market square was designed to control activity to be able to collect taxes. If we were to transpose our modern financial system architecture back to 1086, London's market would be twenty times the size. Instead of sixty market towns, there may be a handful. If the Normans had gone down the pathway of promoting London as a single market to the exclusion of all sixty other market towns, a possible scenario is that poverty and civil disruption would grow outside of London. To counteract this the Normans may have needed to establish aid programs to distribute food to areas of poverty (or more likely violence). To encourage economic activity the Normans could have created an institution offering loans at concessional rates of interest. That institution would be geographically based in London, and because of the time it would have taken to negotiate a transaction would have strong incentives to arrange larger transactions. In this slightly ridiculous 'parallel universe', London's vibrant economy would be contrasted with the stagnant economy in the rest of England. The point here is that an international sustainable development architecture, even if it does focus on sustainable development through the Sustainable Development Goals, *is ridiculous* if it principally focuses on large scale transactions and does not support the development of localized markets. And yet that is how our international financial system architecture works. A question is why isn't there a greater focus on the importance of financial system markets for sustainable development? There is the tendency to forget the linkages between a market and a local economy. Research on this topic dates back almost eighty years with Jospeh Schumpter's finding in 1934 that the system for allocating capital has a substantial impact on economic growth. Over the last twenty years US economist Ross Levine led a global research renaissance into the subject, finding a strong correlation between financial development and economic growth. According to Patrick Honohan, formally a lead economist at the World Bank, if a country moved from the lowest decile of financial depth (13%) to the highest (75%), it could expect to improve its growth rate significantly by over 4 percent in this model all other things being equal. According to research by Ross Levine and Asli Demirgüç-Kunt, "We are not simply finding that finance accelerates economic growth which helps the poor. We are finding that finance exerts a disproportionately positive influence on the poor". In a separate paper research by Beck, Demirgüç

Kunt and Levine found that financial development disproportionately helps the disadvantaged citizens of a less developed country. "Greater financial development induces the incomes of the poor to grow faster than average per capita GDP growth, which lowers income inequality. The results indicate that financial development helps the poorest quintile beyond finance's effect on aggregate growth. Indeed, we find that 60% of the impact of financial development on the poorest quintile works through aggregate growth and about 40% operates through reductions in income inequality. While subject to more qualifications because of greater data limitations, we found that greater financial development is associated with poverty alleviation, even when controlling for average growth and other country traits." There are a few reasons why the development of financial depth alleviates poverty. Honohan quotes Li, Squire and Zou (1997) that better financial development can alleviate credit constraints for poorer households, allowing them to make productive investments, for example in human capital. Research by Rajan and Zingales cited in Honahan argues that "a healthy financial system can be a powerful anti-monopoly tool, providing the lubrication for the emergence of competitors that can undermine the power of incumbent firms, and the means for poor households and small-scale producers to escape the tyranny of exploitative middlemen. In contrast, the undeveloped financial system, in their words, can be 'clubby, uncompetitive and conservative'". It has been established that the development of a local financial sector contributes to economic growth and poverty alleviation but what role do equity markets play in alleviating poverty? Ross Levine and Sara Zervos found that stock market liquidity as measured by stock trading relative to the size of the market and economy is positively correlated with current and future rates of economic growth, capital accumulation and productivity growth, even after controlling for economic and political factors. Whilst there is contention about Levine and Zervos' findings, studies of specific markets suggest that there is a very strong relationship between stock market development and economic growth. Support for the argument that stock market development has a strong role to play in economic development comes from Salvatore Capasso in research which argues that "a large body of empirical studies clearly shows that the development of stock markets is strongly and positively correlated with the level of economic development and capital accumulation. This is a solid and uncontroversial result, and it appears to be true across time and for many countries". Despite Jospeh Schumpter's arguments that the system for allocating capital has a substantial impact on economic growth, coupled with recent work by Ross Levine and others on the importance of a financial system on economic development, it is largely the case that a focus on the development of financial markets has disappeared from the international sustainable development agenda. This is a significant missing piece. No one has bothered or got close to creating the Bible for a Sustainable Political Economy? Where is the Ricardo, Malthus, Marx, Engels, Keynes, Galbraith of our times that focus on the intersection between sustainability and the economy? The rise of new institutional structures including the UN backed Principles for Responsible Investment and Sustainable Stock Exchanges Initiative has not (yet) led to a focus on means through stock exchanges in local economies that can be developed. While the links between the development of a nation's financial system and economic growth have been empirically proven, there has been little recent debate as to whether in fact the development of a nation's financial services industry does indeed benefit the poorest in a community. Why is this the case? There may be a fear that supporting the development of financial markets has come to be seen as supporting a sector that is associated with high salaries and questionable practices. It is after all a brave politician who is prepared to support the importance of financial market structures in the face of a global financial crises and ongoing scandals. This brings us to the second question on where should the leadership come from to develop markets? There are two groups that can influence the development of financial markets outside of existing major financial markets—institutional investors and governments. Institutional investors could play a role in supporting local stock exchanges in less developed countries (LDCs). There are many reasons that have been cited as to why investors do not invest in LDC capital markets. Investors may have legitimate concerns about governance, transparency, and corruption in LDCs. These concerns however have not led to sufficient investor engagement to improve governance and transparency and it may not be the primary reason why investors have avoided investment in LDC capital markets. Rather it could be argued that one of the primary reasons that institutional investors have not invested time and resources to engage with improving LDC markets is because of path dependency, which creates a self-reinforcing dynamic to support the status quo. This path dependency of 'doing what we have always done' is supported by strong financial incentives. If for example a sovereign wealth fund (SWF) in a LDC already flows funds to an established financial market, what incentive does an investment manager who is engaged by that fund have to propose solution to develop a local market that could result in a reduction in the flow to their own investment products? Another impediment to the development of LDC markets is that investing is subject to a network effect. If a group of investors collaborate to invest in a market, then it is far more likely that they will all succeed than if they individually decided to go it alone. One of the fundamental challenges with financial institutions is that they are not well structured to collaborate and work in partnership. Concepts such as "investment alpha" are predicated on the basis that one investment manager, through their individual skill, can generate returns that others cannot. Institutional banks are financially motivated to create transactions that leverage relationships. The challenge for both institutional investors and banks is that the development of financial markets in LDCs require sharing of information and establishment of collaborative partnerships. Institutional investors acting alone cannot overcome the lack of liquidity that comes from a group of investors being present in the same market. A lack of liquidity is a self-reinforcing factor that also creates incentives for the best companies in region to migrate to larger markets as soon as they are able—with demonstrated negative impacts on the local market. If investors do act collaboratively, there is the potential to create an environment to support the development of local stock exchanges in LDCs and which in turn creates the conditions for economic development and poverty alleviation. To achieve this, a long-term commitment by institutional investors to invest and support the development of LDCs capital markets would be required. But how could this be achieved? This is an area where the comparatively newly formed international architecture such as the Principles for Responsible Investment and Sustainable Stock Exchanges Initiative have the potential to lead. There could be benefit in establishing a multi-stakeholder forum with the express goal of increasing long-term investments into LDCs based on sustainability principles, through the mechanism of further development of stock exchanges in these countries. There is an opportunity for such a forum to focus on innovation around financial practices. Addressing legitimate impediments to investment can be a focus of such a forum. One area of importance is to overcome illiquidity. The need for liquidity leads institutional investors to support some markets ahead of others, which only exacerbates the absence of liquidity elsewhere. One recent innovation is the partnership between the Economic Commission for Africa (ECA) and PIMCO to set up a Liquidity and Sustainability Facility (LSF) that would lower governments' borrowing costs by increasing the demand for their sovereign bonds.[97] The LSF is designed to replicate the 'repo' market dynamics present in developed markets that facilitate the creation of stable and additional funding sources. Such a forum could include representation from the International Finance Corporation, UN backed Principles for Responsible Investment, World Federation of Exchanges, and UN Global Compact, as well as representatives from LDC exchanges and industry experts from data vendors and leading institutional investors themselves. The second group that can influence leadership to support the development of financial markets are governments. The role that governments have played in establishing and maintaining markets has been discussed. The creation of a market square in a medieval market town was a means through which the local lord could control, and gain fees from, market activity. What role can governments play to support financial markets, given the likely aversion of politicians to be seen to support financial institutions, which may be perceived in a less developed country as supporting the rich?

The answer may lie in the concept of Financial System Impact Regulation outlined earlier in the book. There is the potential for regulatory systems to 'nudge' institutional investors to invest outside of established financial markets based on reducing system risks. For financial system regulators to act, there needs to be coordination through the G20 Sustainable Finance Working Group and increased focus on addressing institutional investor impediments to investing in developing economy markets through a focus on governance and liquidity.

FLOW TO COMMUNITIES

The Gaziantep Region in Turkey has an extensive system of underground water canals known as livas. Kastels are the point where the livas are made publicly available and consist of pools, wells, sitting places, small mosques, water closets and places for bathing that can be considered as form of municipal social service.[98] The importance of water to communities meant that kastels were universally available. Agriculture and permanent settlements across the arid regions of Iran are to this day supported by an ancient qanat system that taps alluvial aquifers using gravity through long underground tunnels called koshkan. The Persian Qanat system is managed communally ensuring equitable access to water.[99]

Despite the valuable role that community infrastructure, including sporting facilities, community centres, parks and libraries play in connecting communities, delivering environment benefits, social wellbeing and facilitating economic opportunities, we have not developed the mechanisms to value and prioritize investment. Community assets can be considered the "forgotten infrastructure". A key differentiator between community assets and economic infrastructure such as telecommunications, energy, and water are the role that they play in a community. Community assets cannot be delivered successfully unless communities are actively involved in determining what it is they need and how it should be delivered. The challenge is that model for funding and financing the establishment and renewal of community assets is in urgent need of reform. In many parts of the world, community assets are predominantly funded out of municipal government budgets or through grant funding by federal governments. Grant funding can be sporadic and not linked to measurable economic, social and environment outcomes. COVID-19 may represent a tipping point for the funding of community assets. The impact of the COVID debt overhang has yet to be felt, but one fear is that budget repair of government exacerbates that amount of grant funding that is available for community assets.

Sport is an area where the dynamics exist to develop new models that open a flow of finance. What is extraordinary about sport is that no single sport is dominant everywhere in the world. Sporting facilities reflect this variety of community interests. The importance of sport is reflected in the SDGs, which passed by resolution adopted by the United Nations General Assembly on September 25, 2015 (RES/70/1). The SDGs include direct references to sport with the UN General Assembly stating, "we recognize the growing contribution of sport to the realization of development and peace in its promotion of tolerance and respect and the contributions it makes to the empowerment of women and of young people, individuals and communities as well as to health, education and social inclusion objectives".[100] A case study is the funding of professional sporting facilities. In the United States, the first baseball game with paid admission was between New York City and Brooklyn, which was held at Fashion Race-Course on Long Island in July 1858. Funding through paid admission of spectators unlocked professional sports. As games attracted larger crowds, grandstands were built. Arguably the first public grandstand was built in 1854 at the Melbourne Cricket Ground, the "G", which is now one of the world's largest stadiums.[101] Professional sports is now a huge industry. According to *Forbes*, the average value of the fifty most valuable sports teams is USD 3.4 billion.[102] Despite the size and dominance of professional sports, governments still provide grants and subsidies. An example is the US Tax Reform Act (TRA86), which effectively required that for a municipal authority to receive a federal subsidy, they must rely on tax revenue unrelated to a sporting stadium for financing, such as general sales taxes, property taxes, income taxes, lotteries, or taxes on alcohol and cigarettes. The result were tourism taxes placed on hotel rooms and rental cars. According to the Brookings Institute, whilst in the first half of the twentieth century most stadiums were financed by the private sector, since 1953, the public has effectively subsidized their development and "absent the subsidies from all levels of government, there would be little incentive for the teams or private investors to finance so many new (and increasingly luxurious) stadiums". Whilst the dominance of professional sports has resulted in an increased demand to build stadiums that can cater to large crowds, community sporting facilities have in contrast needed to rely on grants. Examples include the linkage of lottery schemes to grant funding.

One of the ways in which community assets could be financed is through the development of blended municipal finance markets. Cities around the world have been financing their long-term investment needs through municipal bonds for centuries. The first recorded transaction occurred in Genoa in 1150. The United States municipal bond market, worth USD 3.9 trillion involving 36,000 government and non-government obligors, is the deepest and most active municipal bond market in the world.[103] The market is dominated by tax advantaged retail investors who comprise 70 percent of the market. Outside of the US municipal bond market there are challenges around the development of municipal bond markets. Germany has a private loan market, the Schuldschein-Market, which are loans governed by German law, that are structured in a way that creates some similarities to debt securities. One impediment to the development of the Schuldschein market is that transactions are exempt from the obligation to publish a prospectus under the EU-Prospectus Regulation, and therefore cannot be listed for trading that would make the loans available to a wider group of financial participants. The US and German municipal markets demonstrate that there is appetite from investors to invest in municipal debt, whichever way it is formally structured. One of the impediments to the flow of finance for all is that municipal bond and loan markets themselves are biased towards municipalities with high credit ratings. Municipalities that have strong credit ratings can invest in infrastructure that improves the quality of living for its citizens. This creates a mutually reinforcing dynamic where a growing city can make new investments with the affordability of credit an important factor. A city that may be experiencing population decline, due to factors that can include a shift in industrial activities, is in a never-ending fight to cut costs. An example of the cost of budget cutting is the Michigan city of Flint, which experienced a public health crisis from 2014 to 2019 when in a bid to cut USD 5 million costs from its operations it switched from treated Detroit Water and Sewerage Department water to the Flint River. As a result, 100,000 residents were exposed to elevated lead levels and a Legionnaires' disease outbreak killed twelve people, although the original source of the bacteria was never found. The challenge for many parts of the world is that cities do not have access to municipal bond markets at all. Cities in sub-Saharan Africa have raised less than 1 percent of the US amount since 2004. Only a handful of local governments in Africa have successfully issued municipal bonds, almost all of them in South Africa. Jeremy Gorelick, a lecturer in Emerging Markets Finance at Johns Hopkins University, examines why African cities are not using municipal bonds to raise money for capital projects and attributes the lack of bond issuance not to the municipality or potential investors, but to limiting behaviour of national governments.[104] He cites the example of Kampala and Dakar, which worked to receive investment-grade credit ratings, "but political conflicts between the local and national levels led to Dakar's bond issuance being cancelled at the last minute. And in the case of Kampala, national regulation has capped the city's borrowing at a prohibitively low amount. This limit means that the city cannot borrow enough money to make bond issuance worthwhile".[105] According to Gorelick, "Cities in heavily centralized countries are not provided with autonomy for decision-making. Instead, they are positioned as direct participants within an administrative machine governed by decisions from the capital. Any financial obligation entered by a city in this political ecosystem is viewed as one explicitly guaranteed by the central government".[106] The development of municipal bond markets is impeded by four factors. Firstly, national governments may not support a local municipality developing its capacity to borrow. There are different reasons for this including legitimate concerns that if a city defaults that a sovereign entity may be expected to pick up the debt. Secondly, where municipal bonds and loan markets have developed, they have relied on local investors, either through tax breaks in the case of the US municipal bond market, or through private unlisted contracts through Germany's Schuldschein market. A uniform structure for global sub-sovereign municipal bond markets does not yet exist. Thirdly, the key attributes of bond markets are presence of credit ratings that provide assurance to investors. Credit ratings are not available for sub-sovereign municipalities and are themselves a costly part of established bond markets. Fourthly, bond markets are ideally suited for municipalities or businesses that are seeking large amounts of capital. There is a debate around what is the minimum issuance size for a corporate bond, which is in the vicinity of USD 300 million. Structures have not been established to support small-scale financing needs of cities. There is a need, and an opportunity, to establish blended municipal lending markets that provide communities with access to affordable credit. Core to the establishment of such markets is the ability to structure partnerships in a way that supports the confidence of investors. To understand how partnerships can be built we need to again turn back to history.

Historically, many voluntary organizations raised capital for fixed investments through debentures. There are many examples of the use of debentures to finance community assets. Perhaps the best-known debenture is Wimbledon, which historically used the vehicle to fund capital investment, with debenture holders entitled to seats at Centre Court over the period of the investment. Wimbledon Debentures are now traded on the London Stock Exchange. The United States has a rich history of the use of debentures. In 1776, private investors purchased USD 27 million in government bonds to finance the Revolution.[107] Nation building projects such as the purchase of Louisiana to the building of the Panama Canal were financed through debentures. Franklin D. Roosevelt announced in 1941 the establishment of a Defence Savings Bond to finance the United States involvement in World War II. Examples from Australia include the Mounties Club, which was originally established by a group of locals from the Mount Pritchard community outside of Sydney in the 1920's. As Sydney's suburbs grew and new housing estates were built, community infrastructure often lagged. The club, which now has over 100,000 members, was motivated by the original members who simply wanted to have a beer after work, with the nearest bar then over twenty kilometres away. In an era before sophisticated financial services laws, it was a relatively simple thing to issue debentures, with the local community raising £300 to fund its initial activities. A small-scale example was the use of a debenture by a local council to finance the development of Regents Park in Melbourne's suburb of Edithvale and Aspendale, which in 1922 financed the development of sporting facilities through an informal process that involved the community working with the local council, the council providing the finance and the community repaying the cost overtime. The elements of a modern model are to be found in the way in which community infrastructure was created in the past. The key element that enabled the Edithvale–Aspendale community to finance the development of their community facilities back in 1922 was that firstly that the local municipal authority understood that it had a role to play in supporting, but not controlling stakeholders, and secondly that also had a role to play in providing finance. These two elements, stakeholder partnership and participation in a financial system, have largely disappeared from municipal authorities. As finance has become more complicated municipalities have also steered away from involvement in financial systems. The loss of stakeholder partnerships between municipal authorities and community groups is problematic. Municipal authorities need community clubs and community clubs need municipal authorities. For municipal authorities, clubs bring the energy of volunteers necessary to activate spaces. A football pitch without football is simply open green space. But with a club, that open space is transformed into an active community. A debenture was used by the local council to finance the development of Regents Park in Aspendale.

Today financial services regulations have created an environment where financial services products are licensed. This has created a deep gulf between municipal authorities that participated in what may be called the informal financial system. The focus by financial system participants on large scale transactions has reinforced the gulf between municipal authorities and the finance sector to the point where most employees in a municipal authority have no understanding of the latent potential of municipal finance. Blended municipal finance offers a pathway to bring together community stakeholders, municipal authorities, and financial system participants to finance sustainable development. One tool that blended municipal finance can utilize is securitization. Securitization was born in 1970 with the establishment of the Government National Mortgage Association "Ginnie Mae", which provided the ability to pool mortgage assets into Mortgage-Backed Securities. The technique has been used to parcel up different illiquid assets to make them investable. Aggregating multiple projects can create larger, longer-term investments with a lower overall risk profile that can be suitable investments for pension funds. Securitization reduces the overall cost of the investments, by gaining access to preferential finance rates only available to large institutional investors. A Blended Community Finance Model is a multi-stakeholder approach that aims to create an environment that enables institutional investors to invest in communities at scale through community bonds. The Blended Community Finance Model aims to align the various objectives of local and national authorities, institutional investors, and citizens to deliver environmental and social outcomes for communities. Enabling institutional investors to invest in community assets decreases the dependency on grants, thus generating more social, environmental, economic, and financial wealth in a way that distributes financial and political risk. The model allows for investments to be made across a broad range of communities, thereby reducing the impact of income and social inequity as factors that influence where investments may be made. As a hypothetical example, a blended community bond could bring together thousand separate projects. A total bond of USD 100 to 300 million would then be of sufficient size to attract institutional investors. A blended municipal bond could be issued by a special purpose investment vehicle—a Blended Community Finance Funding Vehicle (BCF). Specifically, the feature of a BCF would include the establishment of a trust structure through which an aggregated portfolio of loans would be sold to institutional investors. Security for loans would consist of credit enhancement that could be provided by local authorities and other stakeholders including members of a local community or professional sporting teams. Credit enhancement would support a higher credit rating for the bond. A governance board would be established under the terms of the Trust Deed. The governance board would be responsible for working with local community groups to develop enhanced accounting and governance practices. Alternatively, banks could directly provide community loans. There is the potential that governments could support bank lending to communities through establishing community loan guarantee programs. Capital market innovations, such as credit enhancement, which have been used in the financial services industry to mitigate project risks and enable financing of a project, are an important element of a blended community loan. In its simplest form, credit enhancement seeks to increase the credit rating/credit worthiness of the financeable aspects of an infrastructure project. The main objective of a credit-enhancement mechanism is to ameliorate the credit quality of infrastructure projects that have already achieved a certain minimum threshold, to attract more private financing for the project. One example of credit enhancement is Partial Credit Guarantees (PCG), which is a mechanism to absorb part or all the debt service default risk of a project, irrespective of the cause of default. There is the potential for credit enhancement to come from stakeholders, including philanthropic community and businesses. A securitized blended community finance loan would be offered to capital markets on commercial terms. In addition to the risk and return equation, these loans would be attractive as impact investments since they would be able to demonstrate very clear social, environment and economic benefits. To attract investors there is a need for a blended community bond to establish a clear set of standards, which would enable investors to understand the impacts of the bond. As impacts will vary by community led project, there is a need to establish standardized reporting at an individual project level to enable aggregation at the bond level. A critical component of the Blended Community Finance Model is the establishment of Community Partnership Agreements (CPAs) as a means by which the obligations of different stakeholders are clearly set out. CPAs are necessary to clearly define the responsibilities of all the parties that must come together to unlock investment and ensure debt repayment under any number of defined scenarios. A CPA would set out the terms by which communities are able to access finance and outline the mechanism by which stakeholders will support community bond repayment or involvement in club revenue generating activities. CPAs would set out strategic long-term development plans of a community facility and mechanisms by which the impact of environmental, social, and economic benefits from investment will be measured and reported.[108] In summary, community infrastructure has become the forgotten infrastructure but is critical for local community development. Mechanisms such as securitization can be applied to open blended municipal bond markets with Community Partnership Agreements providing the mechanism to bring diverse stakeholders together.

FLOW FOR PEOPLE

Consideration of the flow of finance to all would be incomplete without an examination of the importance of employment to provide a flow of income to support households to meet their basic needs. Two core issues impact the flow of finance to individuals. Firstly, do individuals have access to regular employment and secondly, are workers paid at least a minimum wage for the work they do. Debates over the access to and payment for work have a long history. In 1799, Robert Owen famously established the New Lanark textile mill, successfully demonstrating that good treatment of workers was consistent with the productivity and efficiency of business. For financial system participants including banks and investors the flow of income supports the ability of an individual to borrow and to save and invest. The casualization of work, which impacts on the regularity of income, has implications for the products delivered by financial institutions. It is impossible to talk about work without talking about management practices in general. The way human capital is used in an organization constantly evolves and is influenced by technology, regulation, and particular management trends. Human capital is also subject to a range of megatrends that impact on companies. According to a report by UNI, a global federation of trade unions representing 20 million workers,[109] "work is being redefined the world over as a range of forces impact on the shape of the labor market. Job insecurity and poor- quality work are key emerging characteristics for increasing numbers of workers up and down the hierarchy". UNI Global Union have identified mega-trends that are driving change in the labor markets, including weak and uncertain economic performance, demographic shifts, technological transformation and importantly footloose capital and dominant business models. One of the major megatrends facing the global economy is rising inequality. The International Monetary Union states that, "long periods of rising inequality can increase the risk of economic crises, as they may induce the poor to over-borrow from the rich".[110] According to the IMF, there is evidence that since the early 1980s income inequality has risen in many advanced economies and wages have not risen with productivity.[111] Stagnant wages are playing a significant role in widening inequality. The International Labor Organization (ILO) has stated that whilst 90 per cent of ILO Member States have minimum wage policies in place, either statutory or negotiated through collective bargaining, 266 million wage earners are paid less than the minimum wage, either because they are not legally covered or because of non-compliance.[112] A significant question is, what responsibility do financial systems have to contribute to best practice employment practices? Commentators including John C. Bogle and David Weil have argued that institutional investment practices have had an influence at a system level. Founder of Vanguard Group John C. Bogle has stated he believes that system structure has influenced corporate behaviour.[113] David Weil argues that the emergence of what he calls a fissured workplace[114] was driven by institutional investors that focused on outsourcing business functions that were regarded as "non-core". One of the implications of Weil's work is the need for investors to consider how their behaviour impacts on the overall system and whether dominant investment practices may have an impact on the diversity of corporate thinking. If investors can influence the business models of corporations, which in turn can impact on human capital management practices, is it possible to do so in a way that promotes human centred work practices? For financial system participants, there is a question as to how human capital impacts risk of investment and finance decisions. Human capital risks that financial institutions are exposed to include:

Modern Slavery: Modern slavery practices, such as servitude and forced labor is illustrated by a variety of exploitative practices, such as high-risk employment; forced begging, prostitution, and marriage; bonded labor and recruitment into crime. Today the exploitative practices associated with slavery are most prevalent in those countries or regions where the rule of law within states has broken down and where there is a prevalence of conflict and economic stagnation. According to The International Trade Union Confederation (ITUC), "The vast majority of workers, namely migrant workers, in the Gulf countries are excluded from basic protections under the labor laws, including the right to freedom of association and to bargain collectively. This, in tandem with repressive sponsorship laws, systematically exposes these workers to forced labor". A challenge for an investor who holds a minority share in a large corporation that has layers of suppliers and sub-contractors, is how to influence the supply chain to get to the root of the problem. One mechanism investors use is to assess whether a company has human rights policies in place internally and the degree to which these policies are implemented. An independent third-party audit of implementation can support that assessment. As an example, the Council on Ethics to the Norwegian Government Pension Fund Global (GPFG) has a mandate from the Norwegian Ministry of Finance to actively uncover cases of grossly unethical behaviour in portfolio companies. In the Council's view, the threshold for what may be regarded as violations of norms is lower if it concerns a company's own operations (for instance a producer of goods) than if a company is linked to such violations through a commercial relationship with a third party (for instance a buyer of products). As the employer, a company has an independent responsibility for its employees and for preventing any infringement of their rights. Investors may engage directly or indirectly around modern slavery practices and may consider how and where they are likely to obtain reliable data, which again might affect which regions are regularly surveyed. NGOs including Verite and Humanity United are a source of independent information and data.[115]

Child labor: Child labor has emerged as a significant financial risk as globalization has opened supply chains. Child labor is very costly for society.

When a child works instead of attending school, they are deprived of the opportunity to develop skills that can enable them to earn income throughout their life. This perpetuates a cycle of poverty. According to Humanity United, "When children are recruited to work, whether as domestic servants, brick moulders, or miners, it is typically because they are considered easier to control and intimidate than adults. They demand less pay, if any, and are not equipped to stand up for their rights. As a result, they are disproportionately more vulnerable to violence, abuse, and exploitation".[116] Overall, one hundred seventy-nine countries have ratified the ILO Convention on the Worst Forms of Child Labor and several industries have developed specific programs to address child labor in their supply chain. An example is the cocoa industry, which in 2001 had agreed to the Harkin-Engel Protocol with the aim of eradicating the worst forms of child labor in the production of cocoa. The International Cocoa Initiative was then formed under the protocol's auspices in 2002 but has still not eliminated child labor from the supply chain. As with modern slavery, child labor is considered an investment risk for many institutional investors. A universal owner with a long-term outlook will be concerned with investment sectors and geographies where there is a high risk of child labor. Institutional investors like APG and NBIM have actively sought ways of addressing child labor at portfolio company level over many years. The underlying expectation is that companies respect children's rights in line with the United Nations Guiding Principles and incorporate children's rights in strategic planning, risk management and reporting.

Sexual harassment: When Oprah, repeated three times the words "Their time is up!" in her thank you speech at the 2018 Golden Globes, the "Me Too" campaign reached a tipping point. The "Me Too" campaign is an example of the power of social media to create new movements with long term implications for businesses and investors. Following the public revelations of sexual misconduct allegations against Harvey Weinstein, actress Alyssa Milano tweeted on October 15, 2017: "If all the women who have been sexually harassed or assaulted wrote 'Me too' as a status, we might give people a sense of the magnitude of the problem." Since then, millions of tweets have been made using the "Me Too" hashtag. According to the Equal Employment Opportunity Commission, one in four women in the US experiences sexual harassment at work.[117] Investment risk may manifest through litigation or reputational damage from scandals playing out in the public domain.

Minimum wage and wage theft: Walmart and McDonald's are two companies that have responded in the last few years to community-based campaigns to increase minimum wages. Walmart increased the pay of 500,000 full-time and part-time US employees to USD 9.00 an hour, with a further increase to USD 10.00 an hour by February 2016, at a cost of USD 1 billion. In the US, McDonalds was subject to a nation-wide community campaign led by Service Employees International Union (SEIU), ultimately announcing it would raise the average hourly rate for workers at restaurants it owns to USD 9.90 from USD 9.01 starting July 2015, with average wages climbing above USD 10 per hour by the end of 2016. Whilst we have seen the development of minimum wage campaigns in jurisdictions such as the UK and US, a key issue that has emerged is whether employees are paid their full entitlements. Companies that operate franchise structures have had revelations that workers have been paid well below legal entitlements.

Whilst financial system participants are exposed to specific human capital risks, human capital is also core to value creation. The way to create value out of human capital is the subject of significant discussion amongst management practitioners. One of the challenges, as Richard D'Aveni identified in 1994 is that business is subject to 'hyper-competition'. A company that may have a competitive advantage today may find that it disappears tomorrow, incentivising corporations to focus on a continual process of improvement and change. Geoffrey Matthews and Linda Holbeche in their book *Engaged: Unleashing Your Organization's Potential Through Employee Engagement*, argue that: "To succeed in today's knowledge- or service-based economies, it's not enough to have flexible business models, structures, and processes. People are the source of production and of innovation".[118]

Matthews and Holbeche's central argument is that in a fast-changing economy, businesses need to ensure their employees are engaged. Whilst they acknowledge it is difficult to find irrefutable proof that engagement leads directly to performance improvements, they present research in support of their argument including studies that demonstrate the financial impact of employee engagement.[119] In the last fifteen years we have seen the emergence of responsible investment as a distinct investment discipline. An issue that is particularly important to the incorporation of human capital into investment practices is the concept of materiality. Human capital management may be an important issue for many reasons including the impact of employment on the fabric of society. But are human capital issues considered material to investment decision-making? Amongst different stakeholders there are different definitions on what is considered material, and how to assess materiality. The Global Reporting Initiative defines materiality in respect to sustainability reporting to "reflect the reporting organization's significant economic, environmental, and social impacts; or substantively influence the assessments and decisions of stakeholders". Aaron Bernstein and Larry Beeferman's paper, *The Materiality of Human Capital to Corporate Financial Performance* found evidence that human factors are material to investors. From a survey of ninety-two empirical studies that examined the relationship between Human Resources (HR) polices and financial outcomes, Bernstein and Beeferman found that: "There is sufficient evidence of human capital materiality to financial performance to warrant inclusion in standard investment analysis".[120] However, whilst empirical evidence that human capital is material for investors, Bernstein and Beeferman acknowledged that integrating human capital into investment decision-making was problematic because of a lack of comparable data and a "lack of consensus over which combinations of policies have the most impact on financial outcomes".[121] Bernstein and Beeferman's argument is that: "Investors need an overview of a firm's HR strategy that explains which bundle of policies it employs and why (for each policy and in relation to one another), and how they fit into the overall HR and business strategy". Whilst there are different ways of expressing materiality, the common denominator is that materiality involves significant impact over the short- or long-term. Because it is impossible to operate a company without human capital, then it is unquestionably material. For financial system participants to be able to incorporate human capital into investment and finance practices there is a need for quality reporting on human capital by companies. One of the issues that has been identified by investors is the need for better reporting of human capital. International initiatives that are focused on improving human capital disclosure include the Global Reporting Initiative (GRI), Human Capital Management Coalition and Workforce Disclosure Initiative. GRI Standards are structured as a set of thirty-six GRI Sustainability Reporting Standards that are regularly updated. The Human Capital Management Coalition (HCM Coalition) is a global group of thirty-five institutional investors representing over USD 6.6 trillion in assets.[122] The approach of the Coalition is to: "Elevate human capital management as a critical component in company performance. The Coalition engages companies and other market participants with the aim of understanding and improving how human capital management contributes to the creation of long-term shareholder value". The Workforce Disclosure Initiative (WDI) aims to improve corporate transparency and accountability on workforce issues, provide companies and investors with comprehensive and comparable data and help increase the provision of good jobs worldwide. The WDI investor coalition is made up of fifty-three institutions, with USD 7.5 trillion in assets under management.[123] The Committee on Workers Capital (CWC) is a network that works to educate union pension trustees on responsible investment, monitoring global trends and policies related to corporate and financial market governance. CWC has produced Guidelines for the Evaluation of Workers' Human Rights and Labour Standards, which provide a set of forty-seven key human rights and labor relations indicators across ten themes; workforce composition, social dialogue, workforce participation, supply chain, occupational health and safety (OHS), pay levels, grievance mechanisms, training and development, workplace diversity and pension fund contributions for employees. The International Organization for Standardization (ISO) is a worldwide federation of national standards bodies that develops technical standards through ISO member bodies and Technical Committees. ISO has produced an International Standard ISO/DIS 30414 (Human resource management—Guidelines for human capital reporting for internal and external stakeholders).

The plethora of human capital reporting initiatives is positive. However, because human capital is multi-faceted and dynamic in its evolution, there is a need for financial system participants to consider human capital issues from a holistic perspective. One of the features of human capital risk is that in some circumstances there is an absence of information due to the powerless position that some workers are in. There have been a range of examples of this amongst vulnerable workers in agriculture. The absence of information however does not mean there is an absence of risk. There is an argument that the absence of information may in fact allow poor practices to continue and grow unabated. In our modern society, with the prevalence of social media, it is inevitable that information will eventually flow that exposes poor practice. For financiers, exposure of poor practices has legal implications, particularly in the case of modern slavery and child work. There is significant evidence that human capital risks are prevalent and impact on the financial system. Human capital risk may not necessarily be accompanied by the presence of information to assess the degree of risk. This is particularly the case with human rights risks where there is a fundamental power imbalance that acts as a deterrent for human rights abuse victims to report. Human capital risks may manifest themselves through individual examples of employee treatment, or individual human rights violations. The challenge with individual cases, however high profile they may be, is that they may not be repeated in the same form and may not be regarded as "material" according to definitions of materiality that are commonly used by investors. Human capital risks may also be concentrated in small cap companies where the larger institutional investors may not actively invest. While some human capital risks are clearly captured in international and national regulation (soft and hard), other risks may not be codified in regulation. That does not mean that those risks do not represent a financial risk. Because a company's business model can create long-term investment and finance risks, financial system participants need to have an active voice on business models prior to risks becoming a reality. For financial system participants, the presence of collective bargaining is an indicator that employees have the capability to have a voice. Many countries have endorsed the ILO's *Right to Organise and Collective Bargaining Convention*. Collective bargaining is a means by which human capital risks can be brought to the attention of representatives that are outside of the employment relationship. Whilst financial system participants may be interested in the outcome of a particular set of collective bargaining discussions, they also have an interest in collective bargaining from a system perspective. Collective bargaining is an indicator which, in the context of other factors, can be used by investors to assess risk. It is therefore in the interest of financial system participants to engage at a system level to ensure that employees have the right to collectively bargain. This includes engaging with governments around labor standards as the flow on effect of poor human capital practices impacts on financial products including payment of insurance payments, mortgages, and contributions to savings plans. Financial system participants need to employ strategies and tools, which in combination can bring about better human capital management at company level. For financial institutions, a Human Capital Strategic Engagement Model offers a mechanism to improve long-term performance, which is based around risk management practices that are commonly used in the corporate sector. The Human Capital Strategic Engagement Model consists of a simple traffic light system to identify risk. Traffic lights are commonly used in risk registers and provide an easy way of identifying the most severe risks. The intention of the Human Capital Strategic Engagement Model is to link into market indicators of human capital performance. Strategic engagement on human capital should be seen from a universal owner perspective. Where focused strategic engagement delivers an outcome in an individual company, or amongst a group of workers such as through achieving zero workplace fatalities, the benefits of engagement will apply to all workers, companies, and financial system participants by improving standards and reducing risk. Financial system participants need to also recognize the need to engage with policymakers who set the rules and regulations around employment. The key questions that should form the basis of human capital engagement by financial institutions, whether to organizations where investors supply debt or equity, or to policymakers are human capital strategy, management of human capital risks including modern slavery and child labor, collective bargaining with employees, casualization, training and professional development and occupational health and safety.

FLOW TO BIODIVERSITY

It is perhaps fitting that a book that began with unpacking the importance of the flow of water to the development of civilization should end by focusing on the importance of water in the context of biodiversity and climate change. We started the book with an explanation that we assumed that you, the reader, have a broad understanding of the risks of uncontrolled and rampant changes to the world's climate, the current state of inequality and the raft of environmental, social and governance (ESG) issues that threaten economies and the fabric of society. The reason to make this assumption was so that we could focus our efforts on finding solutions, rather than simply describing the problems. With biodiversity, however, we break this rule. It may not always be apparent to the naked eye, but eco-systems are on the verge of breakdown. Rather than spending the chapter describing the state of the planet in statistical terms, there is no one better to summarize where the world is at than David Attenborough who in the Foreword of The *Dasgupta Review*[124] states: "We are facing a global crisis. We are totally dependent upon the natural world. It supplies us with every oxygen-laden breath we take and every mouthful of food we eat. But we are currently damaging it so profoundly that many of its natural systems are now on the verge of breakdown. Every other animal living on this planet, of course, is similarly dependent. But in one crucial way, we are different. We can change not just the numbers, but the very anatomy of the animals and plants that live around us. We acquired that ability, doubtless almost unconsciously, some ten thousand years ago, when we had ceased wandering and built settlements for ourselves. It was then that we started to modify other animals and plants. At first, doubtless, we did so unintentionally. We collected the kinds of seeds that we wanted to eat and took them back to our houses. Some doubtless fell to the ground and sprouted the following season. So over generations, we became farmers. We domesticated animals in a similar way. We brought back the young of those we had hunted, reared them in our settlements and ultimately bred them there. Over many generations, this changed both the bodies and ultimately the characters of the animals on which we depend. We are now so mechanically ingenious that we are able to destroy a rainforest, the most species-rich ecosystem that has ever existed and replace it with plantations of a single species in order to feed burgeoning human populations on the other side of the world. No single species in the whole history of life has ever been so successful or so dominant. Now we are plundering every corner of the world, apparently neither knowing or caring what the consequences might be. Each nation is doing so within its own territories. Those with lands bordering the sea fish not only in their offshore waters but in parts of the ocean so far from land that no single nation can claim them. So now we are stripping every part of both the land and the sea in order to feed our ever-increasing numbers. How has the natural world managed to survive this unrelenting ever-increasing onslaught by a single species? The answer of course, is that many animals have not been able to do so. When Europeans first arrived in southern Africa they found immense herds of antelope and zebra. These are now gone and vast cities stand in their stead. In North America, the passenger pigeon once flourished in such vast flocks that when they migrated, they darkened the skies from horizon to horizon and took days to pass. So, they were hunted without restraint. Today, that species is extinct. Many others that lived in less dramatic and visible ways simply disappeared without the knowledge of most people worldwide and were mourned only by a few naturalists. Nonetheless, in spite of these assaults, the biodiversity of the world is still immense. And therein lies the strength that has enabled much of its wildlife to survive until now. Economists understand the wisdom of spreading their investments across a wide range of activities. It enables them to withstand disasters that may strike any one particular asset. The same is true in the natural world. If conditions change, either climatically or as a consequence of a new development in the never-ending competition between species, the ecosystem as a whole is able to maintain its vigour. But consider the following facts. Today, we ourselves, together with the livestock we rear for food, constitute 96% of the mass of all mammals on the planet. Only 4% is everything else – from elephants to badgers, from moose to monkeys. And 70% of all birds alive at this moment are poultry – mostly chickens for us to eat. We are destroying biodiversity, the very characteristic that until recently enabled the natural world to flourish so abundantly. If we continue this damage, whole ecosystems will collapse. That is now a real risk. Putting things right will take collaborative action by every nation on earth. It will require international agreements to change our ways. Each ecosystem has its own vulnerabilities and requires its own solutions. There has to be a universally shared understanding of how these systems work, and how those that have been damaged can be brought back to health".

According to the Intergovernmental Science-Policy Platform on Biodiversity and Ecosystem Services (IPBES), which is based on the United Nations Intergovernmental Panel on Climate Change (UN IPCC) model of providing international science-based assessments, nature, and its vital contributions to people, which together embody biodiversity and ecosystem functions and services, are deteriorating worldwide.[125] IPBES highlight the impact of human actions that are threatening more species with global extinction now than ever before. The 2019 IPBES global assessment states: "An average of around 25 per cent of species in assessed animal and plant groups are threatened, suggesting that around 1 million species already face extinction, many within decades, unless action is taken to reduce the intensity of drivers of biodiversity loss. Without such action, there will be a further acceleration in the global rate of species extinction, which is already at least tens to hundreds of times higher than it has averaged over the past 10 million years".[126] As ecosystems struggle to deal with ongoing human actions such as land clearing, climate change is posing an existential threat for many species. The International Panel on Climate Change's most recent assessment, Climate Change 2021: The Physical Science Basis,[127] states that: "For every additional increment of global warming, changes in extremes continue to become larger". An area of particular focus for biodiversity is how climate change impacts rainfall patterns. According to the IPCC, "Every additional 0.5 °C of global warming causes clearly discernible increases in the intensity and frequency of hot extremes, including heatwaves (very likely), and heavy precipitation (high confidence), as well as agricultural and ecological droughts in some regions (high confidence). Increases in frequency and intensity of hydrological droughts become larger with increasing global warming in some regions (medium confidence). There will be an increasing occurrence of some extreme events unprecedented in the observational record with additional global warming, even at 1.5 °C of global warming. Projected percentage changes in frequency are higher for rarer events (high confidence)". IPCC argue that: "It is very likely that heavy precipitation events will intensify and become more frequent in most regions with additional global warming. At the global scale, extreme daily precipitation events are projected to intensify by about 7% for each 1 °C of global warming (high confidence). The proportion of intense tropical cyclones (categories 4-5) and peak wind speeds of the most intense tropical cyclones are projected to increase at the global scale with increasing global warming (high confidence)." Living in Bangkok making the professional transition from journalism to business, Paul Clements Hunt's first direct involvement around the challenges of climate change was in 1992. What was then the Oxford University Environmental Change Unit (ECU) had presented a paper in the Thai capital exploring the impacts of temperature rise on the productivity of agricultural communities in Thailand, Malaysia, and Indonesia. One statistic was that at 42 degrees centigrade productivity of agricultural out-growers declines precipitously. Turned into a feature for the UK magazine, *New Scientist*, Paul dove deep into two things: Firstly, CERCLA/ Superfund (Comprehensive Environmental Response, Compensation, and Liability Act of 1980); and secondly, the Antarctic Environmental Protection Treaty. Paul says, "I remember sitting in 1992 in the Buddha-shrine like office of a very shrewd, extremely wealthy Thai banking Chair/CEO in Bangkok while, as a twenty-six-year-old environmental start up entrepreneur, I extolled on links between finance and the foul, polluted state of the Chao Phraya River he used to swim in as a boy where the fish were so abundant you could 'pluck them out of the water'. He listened attentively and patiently and counselled wisely, 'I believe now this is for Central Banks and Prime Ministers'".

For one iconic species, Australia's platypus, climate change represents a threat to survival. For the first time in its 4-million-year history, in 2021 the platypus was officially listed as vulnerable in the state of Victoria, Australia in which it thrived before European settlement.[128] Platypus[129] are entirely dependent on aquatic ecosystems. The species occurs in a variety of water bodies including rivers, creeks, lakes, as well as man-made dams and reservoirs where there is reliable surface water. Platypuses are seasonal breeders with courtship and mating generally occurring in early spring, and independent juveniles emerging from burrows in late summer. The breeding season is typically from August to the end of November, with young emerging from their nest and weaning in late summer. Platypuses are monotremes, mammals that lay eggs rather than bearing live young. The female platypus lays one to three eggs and will suckle the young for three to four months prior to them emerging from the nest. In addition to ongoing land use changes that impact platypus habitat, the challenge that climate change poses for the platypus is the variability of rainfall. Platypuses rely on reliable surface water to breed. If the conditions are not right, then the platypus will not breed every season. According to the Australian Government's latest State of the Climate 2020 report,[130] Australia's climate has already warmed by over 1 °C since 1960. The warmest year on record was 2019, with the seven years from 2013 to 2019 all ranking in the nine warmest years. It is however the shifting weather patterns that threaten the platypus. The southeast of the continent is drying out whilst northern Australia has been wetter across all seasons. When rain does come, we are seeing an increase in the intensity of heavy rainfall events. Australia's Bureau of Meteorology State of the Climate 2020 report states: "As the climate warms, heavy rainfall events are expected to continue to become more intense. A warmer atmosphere can hold more water vapour than a cooler atmosphere, and this relationship alone can increase moisture in the atmosphere by 7 per cent per degree of global warming. This can cause an increased likelihood of heavy rainfall events. Increased atmospheric moisture can also provide more energy for some processes that generate extreme rainfall events, which further increases the likelihood of heavy rainfall due to global warming".[131] If the planet experiences 1.5 °C of global warming, then we can expect that temperatures over landmass will be higher than over water. There is the potential that temperatures on a hot summer's day across southeast Australia may range between 40-45 °C. High temperatures themselves represent a threat for some species. Flying foxes for instance are unable to survive when temperatures exceeded 42 °C. Estimates are that 23,000 flying foxes died in two days of extreme heat in Queensland in 2014.[132] For the platypus, high temperatures result in high rates of evapotranspiration, which reduces water in creeks, rivers, and lakes. It is not just higher temperatures that pose a threat. Flash flooding, which we can expect in a 1.5 °C world, has the potential to washout platypus nesting burrows. The threat to the platypus will not take place at some distant date in the future. It is today. It is possible that at any time in the next years we can envisage a spring flash flood followed by a string of 45 °C+ days. In this environment, the platypus will not breed. We have focused on the platypus because it is such an iconic species. Botanist Sir Joseph Banks, who accompanied Lieutenant James Cook, captain of HMB Endeavour, on the expedition of the Australian continent claiming the eastern portion of the Australian continent for the British Crown in 1770,[133] believed at first that the platypus must be a hoax. When he did receive a specimen in 1802, he sent it to French Zoologist, Étienne Geoffroy de Saint-Hilaire, at the Muséum d'Histoire Naturelle in Paris who identified it as belonging to the family of monotremes. Napoleon himself examined the specimen.[134] The platypus is however not alone in being threatened due to the impacts of climate change. It is estimated that 6,300 of known species of amphibians, 12 percent of 9,865 bird species, 21 percent of all fish species, 30 percent of invertebrate species and half the globe's 5,491 known mammals are currently under threat.[135] On the positive side there is increasing momentum to recognize the importance of biodiversity and ecosystems through financial systems. There are two developments of note: The Taskforce on Nature-related Financial Disclosures and the Dasgupta Review. The Taskforce on Nature-related Financial Disclosure (TNFD) is a risk management and disclosure framework for organizations, which is currently under development. TNFD received a considerable boost in 2021 with the G20's Sustainable Finance Working Group (SFWG) officially endorsing it in its Sustainable Finance Roadmap. The G20 SFWG, which is discussed earlier in the book has outlined a series of actions that will be driven through International Organizations (IOs). It is expected that TNFD will test and revise a framework in 2022 and consult stakeholders and launch the framework in 2023. The work of TNFD will be supported by other IOs including the Network for Greening the Financial System (NGFS), United Nations Environment Programme Finance Initiative (UNEP FI), OECD and the Coalition of Finance Ministers for Climate Action (CFMCA) who will focus on research on how nature-related financial risks manifest, how biodiversity loss transmits to financial risks and the impact of biodiversity risks in financial markets. TNFD may be particularly important for bond markets. Governments themselves, as well as municipal authorities owned and controlled by governments, rely on bond markets to raise capital to meet needs. If governments take a lead in disclosing nature-related risks through their own bond market dealings, this would have a major impact on driving acceptance of nature-related financial risks into financial market practices.

The Dasgupta Review[136] published in February 2021 represents a critical step forward in momentum. The Report's core argument is that the economics of biodiversity is the economics of the entire biosphere which, using the language of finance, in turn becomes a study in portfolio management. The importance of the Dasgupta Review is that it formally brings biodiversity into the language of economics. Partha Dasgupta argues that nature is more than a mere economic good. "Nature nurtures and nourishes us, so we will think of assets as durable entities that not only have use value, but may also have intrinsic worth … Whether as farmers or fishers, foresters or miners, households or companies, governments, or communities, we manage the assets to which we have access, in line with our motivations as best as we can. But the best each of us is able to achieve with our portfolios may nevertheless result in a massive collective failure to manage the global portfolio of all our assets."[137] Bringing biodiversity formally into the economics profession enables the development of an understanding of aspects of biodiversity from the perspective of supply and demand. An example is water, which underpins so much of the planet's biodiversity. Using the language of economics, the challenge with water is that demand and supply can change rapidly. The variability of rainfall, which is expected to increase because of climate change, can result in a massive shift from excess of supply (flood) to excess of demand (drought). Water as a commodity has four broad stakeholders who all use water for different purposes. Households principally use water for cleaning and drinking but also water gardens and fill swimming pools. Businesses use water for a range of industrial applications which vary in their demands. Farmers use water for agriculture and animal husbandry. Water for biodiversity includes rainfall that sustains plants, feeds streams, creeks, rivers, and lakes and flows into marine environments. When there is an excess of supply of water (flood) the focus is how to limit the damage on property and transmit it quickly and efficiently away from an area. This can involve building infrastructure such as drains, which transmit water quickly away from urban environments which themselves destroy a local ecosystem. When there is an excess of demand for water (drought) this is where different problems arise. Of the four water stakeholders (households, businesses, farming and biodiversity) it is biodiversity which has the least ability to speak for itself when supply for water is scarce. The reality of climate change is that there is increased likelihood that there will be times of water scarcity and times of intense rainfall events. Whilst financial systems cannot alter when and where it rains, there is the potential to reduce conflict amongst stakeholders who have competing interests, and more specifically to guarantee the supply of water for biodiversity through new investment models. To develop a new model for financing biodiversity there is a need to understand how urban water infrastructure was built and financed in the first instance. Every city has its history of building water infrastructure. The development of civilization in Mesopotamia, Egypt, India, and China resulted from harnessing water through canals. Today we take for granted that we can turn on a tap and clean, drinkable water flows. As urban populations have grown, we have secured water by building dams and increasingly through investment in desalinization plants, which convert brackish and saline water into potable water. It is estimated that there are over 15,000 desalinization plants worldwide.[138] Whilst the focus has been on securing water for domestic, industrial, and agricultural needs, we have however not secured water for biodiversity. The cost of the lack of investment is that it is biodiversity that will bear the brunt of the variability of water that results from a changing climate. Examples of this are already occurring. In southeast of Australia during December 2018 and January 2019, three significant fish kill events occurred in the Darling River near Menindee. Up to one million fish died, with Murray cod, silver perch, golden perch, and bony herring the main species affected.[139] The Murray-Darling River Basin serves multiple needs including water for communities and agriculture. The lack of water allocations for biodiversity exposed biodiversity to risks with blue green algae thriving which, when it dies decomposes oxygen levels below critical levels leading to the death of fish.[140] In the face of anticipated changes to climate a significant question is—How can we unlock a flow of finance at scale to make investments that are specifically focused on supporting biodiversity? Establishing Biodiversity Bonds is proposed as a solution. The nature of biodiversity is that each species, and each ecosystem is unique. Understanding the unique needs of each species and each ecosystem is critically important to open a flow of finance for biodiversity. A Biodiversity Bond Market could consist of a diversity of species and ecosystems. Platypus bonds, zebra bonds and orangutan bonds would be available to institutional investors alongside species and ecosystems that may not have the "name recognition" but which are critically important to biodiversity. On first blush a "bear bond" may raise eyebrows on Wall Street, but it would serve a key purpose of drawing attention to what has the potential to become a deep market that can deliver outcomes to ecosystems as well as risk-adjusted returns for institutional investors. A Biodiversity Bond Market will not be borne overnight. Like any market, an essential ingredient to establish a successful market, as opposed to string of disconnected individual transactions, is the need to focus on building integrity. Examples such as the burgeoning green and sustainability bonds market supported through frameworks including the Climate Bonds Initiative and the International Capital Market Association's (ICMA) Sustainability Bond Principles[141] have laid a foundation for innovation in bond markets. One of the reasons why a Biodiversity Bond Market at scale has not developed to date is that biodiversity involves multiple stakeholders who all have a role to play in both minimizing harm to a species or ecosystem, as well as in regeneration. To establish biodiversity bonds there is a need to be able to articulate to financial institutions how a bond would be repaid. A Biodiversity Bond Market would consist of blended biodiversity bonds with partnerships at their core. The "blended" terminology itself recognizes the focus on blended finance that was led by the United Nations (UN) in 2015 through the Addis Ababa Action Agenda (AAAA), which was an outcome of the Third International Conference on Financing for Development.[142] The OECD defines blended finance[143] as "an approach aiming at attracting commercial capital towards projects that benefit society while providing financial returns to investors" and recognizes that "in blended finance, public and private actors come together to work on areas of mutual interest that promote sustainable development". Critical to the success of any individual 'blended biodiversity bond' is an understanding of the unique needs of each species and ecosystem. This requires an understanding of the reasons why a species or ecosystem is under threat. A core part of a biodiversity partnership should therefore be the establishment of mechanisms that bring integrity to financing through the participation of appropriately qualified scientists.

Returning to the platypus, how would finance be used to secure the future of a species in the face of climate change? The answer to this question will be different for every species and depend on local factors. There is a need to understand how the actions of humans have impacted the species. In the years following Napoleon's viewing of the platypus specimen, a European settlement grew on the banks of the Yarra River in Port Phillip Bay, which began to encroach on an ecosystem that had sustained the local Kulin nation for thousands of years. As Melbourne grew, as the settlement came to be known, the town's waste was tipped directly into the Yarra River. It was the gold rush of the 1850's that made this practice unstainable. As population swelled, Melbourne's sewerage coupled with waste from slaughterhouses was pouring straight into the river. By the 1880's Melbourne was commonly referred to as "Smelbourne". Melbourne's geography meant that heavy rainfalls over winter and spring flowed down a myriad of creeks and streams into wetlands, which the Europeans termed swamps. Melbourne's creeks and wetlands provided a rich food bowl for the Wurundjeri and Bunurong peoples of the Kulin Nation. Kooyang in late summer was known as the season of eels. The seasonal rainfalls also sustained the local platypus population, which was able to move along creek beds and wetlands to breed. In 1873, the Victorian Government responded to the smell and disease, which had become rampant, by holding a Royal Commission on Low Lying Lands, which then led to the establishment in 1891 of the Melbourne and Metropolitan Board of Works (MMBW). The MMBW built dams to capture Melbourne's variable rainfall and piped sewerage to be treated in the then distant town of Werribee. The MMBW also began the process of 'ridding Melbourne of its swamps' by turning creeks and streams into drainage channels, which transported water as quickly as possible to Port Phillip Bay. The result was not surprisingly that the platypus retreated to the upper reaches of the Yarra out of reach of Melbourne's sprawling suburbs. Whilst the "Smelbourne" era is now well past, the legacy of the drainage channels remains. Melbourne Water, the government owned water utility, which is responsible for managing Melbourne's water catchments, is working with a wide range of stakeholders to deliver 'daylighting' projects. Daylighting involves bringing the flow of waterways out of underground concrete pipes and replacing with an open, flowing channel that more closely resembles the original shape and form of creeks.[144] The projects also involve construction of new habitats for threatened fish species as well as focusing on pollution prevention and managing uncontrolled sewage spills. An exciting innovation is that Melbourne Water, together with Yarra Ranges Council and South-East Water are developing a smart rainwater tank using "Tank Talk' flow control technology that enables water to be released remotely to the creek network. The flow of water into creeks at critical times aims to support stream health, which can support platypus breeding.[145] Over the last one hundred ninety years since Melbourne was settled, things have come full circle. There is an emerging understanding that it is possible to have an urban settlement and have a vibrant ecosystem at the same time. An age-old challenge however remains. And that is how to finance the regeneration of habitat whilst investing at scale in new technology that can address the variability of rainfall, which promises to get worse as the impacts of climate change take a grip. The elements of a Platypus Bond all exist. There is a clear program of work that involves daylighting creek beds and investing in smart tanks. There is clear science that supports the need for investment. The question is how to catalyse the finance that can unlock investments that support the platypus and other species. We would argue that there is a logic that water utilities take on the finance role. Water utilities, as the history of New York's Croton Aqueduct demonstrated, have the advantage of established corporate structures and stable ownership that can withstand short-term shocks. In the case of Melbourne, water utilities are owned by the Victorian Government and have the capability to access financial markets through Treasury Corp Victoria. The example of the potential for a scalable Platypus Bond managed by water utilities leads us to a core conclusion, which is that when it comes to the urgent financing of biodiversity there is an opportunity for water utilities globally to take on the responsibility. There are many cases we can cite where water utilities are already taking on responsibilities for biodiversity. There is a logic that water utilities globally collaborate to support the establishment of a Biodiversity Bond Initiative, which would have the objective of establishing a Biodiversity Bond Market that scales the financing of biodiversity.

FLOW, COLLABORATION, TRUST AND EMPATHY

Babylon's ancient Code of Hammurabi was one of the earliest written legal codes. Proclaimed by the Babylonian king Hammurabi, who reigned from 1792 to 1750 BC,[146] amongst the Code's rules lay the foundations of banking. The Code states:

> "*Clause 122. If anyone give another silver, gold, or anything else to keep, he shall show everything to some witness, draw up a contract, and then hand it over for safe keeping.*
>
> *Clause 123. If he turn it over for safe keeping without witness or contract, and if he to whom it was given deny it, then he has no legitimate claim.*
>
> *Clause 124. If anyone deliver silver, gold, or anything else to another for safe keeping, before a witness, but he deny it, he shall be brought before a judge, and all that he has denied he shall pay in full.*
>
> *Clause 125. If anyone place his property with another for safe keeping, and there, either through thieves or robbers, his property and the property of the other man be lost, the owner of the house, through whose neglect the loss took place, shall compensate the owner for all that was given to him in charge. But the owner of*

the house shall try to follow up and recover his property, and take it away from the thief."

Financial systems have developed a long way since the Code of Hammurabi. One of the key elements of the Code however remains the same. Trust. We have outlined a series of practical and implementable ideas in this book that can be achieved without tortuous global negotiations or legislative change. In the end though delivering change is not about the ideas. It is about the willingness to collaborate, the need to build trust, and at core the need for empathy. The world today is more connected than ever before. With the invention and proliferation of the internet, the increasing ease of international travel (with the exception of recent COVID restrictions), the massive market penetration of mobile phones, and the slew of social media and information sharing platforms available today, the most unlikely corners of the globe can connect, communicate, build and transact in just a fraction of a moment. While connectivity is a key factor in creating an inclusive globe, the type of communication and information that is being transferred is not always pure and positive, and therefore requires careful consideration going forward. Every action, or even every lack of action, has a resulting impact—this has been increasingly obvious over the last decade or two as the fragility of our interconnected global ecosystem becomes more and more visible. These realizations are vital and should not be forgotten nor result in complacency or desensitization. As Graham Turner says, "Vested interests and corrupt politicians combined with a population happy to deny problems overwhelm those that are trying to promulgate truth and facts". All the citizens of earth are in this closed system together, and everything needs to be done to ensure a humane life for all. It must also be realized that all creatures should live here in harmony with each other and the environment. For too long, the narrative has been one of disregard thy neighbour and look after oneself. Yet, as we become increasingly secluded on a planet of increasing population, so a collaborative approach to our future becomes increasingly practical and possible even appealing. The challenges we face are enormous and when viewed in their entirety might seem clearly insurmountable, but our biggest challenge is change itself. Change usually entails some form of sacrifice and having less instead of the more we constantly strive for seems somewhat counterintuitive. There is clearly much change happening below the surface level and the world is ablaze with environmental, social, and financial issues being brought to the fore. There is also a great amount of excitement across the sustainability movement as policy changes are finally being delivered in all forms and varieties. While this is great news it seems undeniable that we are a long way behind on the real change that needs to take place—culture change. The way in which we think and behave can change faster than any policy can be implemented, provided it is what we choose to do. Can we have our cake and eat it? Can we continue to poison the river that gives us drinking water? If our good actions outweigh our bad actions (not necessarily by the same people), does that make everything ok? Are we content to live in a poison filled system, or would we be better off with a 'first do no harm' outlook? The major requirement to rejuvenate the concept of community is the flow of empathy. There is already clearly much compassion and consideration abound, but it is all too easy for business to continue as usual and responsibilities to be handed from one generation to the next. It is evident that each subsequent generation is growing more impatient and less impressed with the view of the future. The number of companies being brought to book simply due to public outcry is commendable, and it is often the youth driving these initiatives. Small bands of naysayers are however, simply not enough to take on the enormity of issues we need to deal with in the coming decade, especially in the face of complacency. As COVID has shown us, we cannot simply think of ourselves and still believe that everything will turn out fine. If we do not seek solutions for all of society's ills and indeed for all of society, then all will be impacted by the consequences sooner or later. Changes will come one way or another; we can either be masters of the future, or victims of it. The responsibility that comes with power is not merely reserved for superheroes; rather it applies to all of us, no matter how little power we may possess. At the core of this responsibility is empathy, perhaps not necessarily to the point of altruism, but certainly in the sense of the flow of positive humanity from an area of greater concentration to one more in need, whatever the conditions may be. This flow of empathy and humanity will require a culture change that promotes a more harmonious narrative. A narrative more focused on a sustainable, conservative, and considerate community function. Even though many of the changes that need to happen can in fact happen overnight if given a conducive environment; changing the narratives that have been engrained in society, to increase the flows of empathy, is slightly more complicated and involved.

The term community broadly means a group of people with something in common. It may seem far-fetched to imagine a community as anything more than a local neighbourhood or group of people living in a particular area, but as we are witnessing with things such as viruses or the internet or international travel, our community is global. We no longer exist in a separated world, or at least now we can see that. The sooner this fact is realized and acknowledged, the compassion and empathy will be allowed to flow as it should.

ENDNOTES

1 The Financial Services Group of Livery Companies was founded in 2006 to coordinate the efforts of its members in supporting the Lord Mayor, the Court of Aldermen and the City of London Corporation in promoting the City of London financial and business services sector. https://www.liverycommittee.org/about/livery-companies-and-guilds/financial-services-group/

2 Walter Bagehot, Lombard Street: A Description of the Money Market, 1873

3 UN Sustainable Development Goals, Available at https://sdgs.un.org/goals

4 "Timid Capital" is a term first coined by The Blended Capital Group to describe the self-limiting deep pools of G7/G20/OCED investment funds that rule out frontier market opportunities on an ex-ante basis with little or no reference given to changing geo-politics, policies, opportunities and the demographic bounce underway for many of these countries.

5 See https://www.theguardian.com/cities/2019/jun/19/gaziantep-turkish-city-successfully-absorbed-half-a-million-migrants-from-syria

6 UN Development Program Turkey, The Gaziantep Declaration Calls for Transition From Emergency to Resilience Approach in Migration and Displacement Responses, November 27, 2019, Available at https://www.tr.undp.org/content/turkey/en/home/presscenter/pressreleases/2019/11/gaziantep-declaration.html

7 Paul Clements Hunt moderated the Forum. Gordon Noble was a speaker.

8 UNHCR, Available at https://www.unhcr.org/en-au/figures-at-a-glance.html

9 See https://www.islamic-relief.org/category/strategic-business-units/islamic-social-finance-strategic-business-units/waqf-endowment/#:~:text=Waqf%20(Arabic%20for%20endowment)%20is,serves%20specific%20categories%20of%20beneficiaries.

10 UNESCO, The Underground Water Structures in Gaziantep; Livas' and Kastels, Available at https://whc.unesco.org/fr/listesindicatives/6345/

11 David Graeber, Debt: The First 5,000 Years, 2011

12 IMF, Fiscal Monitor, 2020

13 Karin Strohecker, IIF: Global debt levels decline for the first time in 2-1/2 years, May 13, 2021, Reuters, Available at https://www.reuters.com/article/global-debt-iif-idUSL1N2N00ZU

14 World Federation of Exchanges, 2020 Market Highlights, Available at https://www.world-exchanges.org/storage/app/media/FH.FY%202020%20Market%20Highlights%20v9.pdf

15 Eddershaw, David, Chipping Norton – the story of a market town, Poundstone Press, 2006

16 Lodewijk Petram, The World's First Stock Exchange, New York, Columbia University Press, 2014, Available at https://www.worldsfirststockexchange.com/2020/11/02/the-oldest-share/

17 Lodewijk Petram, The world's first IPO, October 15, 2020, Available at https://www.worldsfirststockexchange.com/2020/10/15/the-worlds-first-ipo/

18 Lodewijk Petram, The World's First Stock Exchange, New York, Columbia University Press, 2014, Available at https://www.worldsfirststockexchange.com/2020/11/02/the-oldest-share/

19 Lodewijk Petram, The VOC and Amsterdam's first exchange building, November 17, 2020, Available at https://www.worldsfirststockexchange.com/2020/11/17/the-voc-and-amsterdams-first-exchange-building/

20 William Dalrymple, The Anarchy: The Relentless Rise of the East India Company, 2019

21 Antipodean Books, Maps & Prints, Course of the Exchange, & C. London, Tuesday, August 27, 1776. London Stock Exchange broadsheet, Available at https://www.antipodean.com/pages/books/23268/sister-of-the-late-john-castaing/course-of-the-exchange-c-london-tuesday-august-27-1776-london-stock-exchange-broadsheet?soldItem=true; Ben Johnson, English Coffeehouses, Penny Universities, Historic UK, Available at https://www.historic-uk.com/CultureUK/English-Coffeehouses-Penny-Universities/

22 Goshen, Z. & Parchom Ovsky, G. (2006). The essential role of securities regulation. Duke Law Journal, p. 55, No. 4.

23 Goshen, Z. & Parchom Ovsky, G. (2006). The essential role of securities regulation. Duke Law Journal, p. 55, No. 4.

24 Lars Boerner, Department of Economic History, London School of Economics, Economic History Working Papers, No. 242/2016, Medieval Market Making Brokerage Regulations In Central Western Europe, ca 1250-1700, June 2016.

25 Cressey, D. R. (1953). Other People's money: A study in the social psychology of embezzlement, Free Press.

26 Austin, Janet. (2016). What exactly is market integrity? An analysis of one of the core objectives of securities regulation. 2017 8 (2) William & Mary Business Law Review 215. Available at SSRN: https://ssrn.com/abstract=2814986 or https://doi.org/10.2139/ssrn.2814986

27 World Federation of Exchanges, 2020 Market Highlights, Available at https://www.world-exchanges.org/storage/app/media/FH.FY%202020%20Market%20Highlights%20v9.pdf

28 Peter Drucker, The Pension Fund Revolution, 1976, revised 1995, p. 88

29 Peter Drucker, The Pension Fund Revolution, 1976, revised 1995, p. 71

30 Peter Drucker, The Pension Fund Revolution, 1976, revised 1995, p. 213

31 Peter Drucker, The Pension Fund Revolution, 1976, revised 1995, p. 221

32 McKinsey & Company, Benchmarking of GPFG management costs, Report for the Norwegian Ministry of Finance, November 2017, Available at https://www.regjeringen.no/contentassets/72ef8a27cca-c441086a53a55b26c2388/171117-benchmarking-of-gpfg-management-costs-vf.pdf

33 Principles for Responsible Investment, How can a passive investor be a responsible investor? a PRI Discussion Paper, 2019

34 Financial Times, Global passive assets hit $15tn as ETF boom heats up, May 10, 2021, https://www.ft.com/content/7d5c2468-619c-4c4b-b3e7-b0da015e939d

35 Roger D. Hansen, Water Wheels, Available at http://www.waterhistory.org/histories/waterwheels/

36 Frank W. Geels, Technological transitions as evolutionary reconfiguration processes: a multi-level perspective and a case-study, Centre for Studies of Science, Technology and Society, University of Twente, Research Policy 31 (2002) 1257–127

37 H. L. Barber, Story of the Automobile: Its History and Development from 1760 to 1917, A.J. Munson & Co, 1917

38 Strong winter dust storms may have caused the collapse of the Akkadian Empire, Science Daily, October 24, 2019, Available at https://www.sciencedaily.com/releases/2019/10/191024093606.htm

39 Stefan Lovgren, Angkor Wat's Collapse From Climate Change Has Lessons for Today, National Geographic, April 5, 2017, Available at https://www.nationalgeographic.com/science/article/angkor-wat-civilization-collapsed-floods-drought-climate-change

40 Sean Fleming, Climate change helped destroy these four ancient civilisations, March 29, 2019, World Economic Forum, Available at https://www.weforum.org/agenda/2019/03/our-turn-next-a-brief-history-of-civilizations-that-fell-because-of-climate-change/

41 Achieving Sustainable Growth, Wealth Creation and Poverty Reduction, Presentation to the UN Secretary General's High Level Panel on Sustainability by Rt Hon Gordon Brown MP, Sunday, September 18, 2011.

42 Lenses and Clocks: Financial stability and systemic, July 2012, UNEP FI, Available at https://www.unepfi.org/publications/general-publications/lenses-and-clocks-financial-stability-and-systemic-risks/

43 United Nations, Inter-agency Task Force on Financing for Development, Financing for Sustainable Development Report 2021.

44 Niall Ferguson, Doom: The Politics of Catastrophe, p. 13

45 Niall Ferguson, Doom: The Politics of Catastrophe, p. 14

46 John Naisbitt, Megatrends: Ten New Directions Transforming Our Lives, Warner Books, 1982

47 Terje Tvedt, The Nile: History's Greatest River, 2021

48 Philippe Aghion, Céline Antonin, Simon Bunel and Jodie Cohen-Tanugi, The Power of Creative Destruction: Economic Upheaval and the Wealth of Nations, 2021

49 Federal Reserve Bank of New York, Kevin Stiroh to Step Down as Head of New York Fed Supervision to Assume New System Leadership Role at Board of Governors on Climate, January 25, 2021, Available at https://www.newyorkfed.org/newsevents/news/aboutthefed/2021/20210125

50 Financial Stability Implications of Climate Change, Remarks by Lael Brainard, Member, Board of Governors of the Federal Reserve System at "Transform Tomorrow Today", Ceres 2021 Conference, Boston, Massachusetts, Available at https://www.federalreserve.gov/newsevents/speech/files/brainard20210323a.pdf

51 FINANCIAL STABILITY OVERSIGHT COUNCIL, Report on Climate-Related Financial Risk, 2021, Available at https://home.treasury.gov/system/files/261/FSOC-Climate-Report.pdf

52 G20 Sustainable Finance Working Group, Available at https://g20sfwg.org/

53 Terje Tvedt, The Nile: History's Greatest River, 2021

54 UNESCO, Persian Caravanserai, Available at https://whc.unesco.org/en/tentativelists/6197/

55 John Major, Silk Road, Spreading Ideas and Innovations, Asia Society, Centre for Global Education, Available at https://asiasociety.org/education/silk-road

56 European Central Bank, Climate-related risks to financial stability, Prepared by Spyros Alogoskoufis, Sante Carbone, Wouter Coussens, Stephan Fahr, Margherita Giuzio, Friderike Kuik, Laura Parisi, Dilyara Salakhova and Martina Spaggiari, Published as part of the Financial Stability Review, May 2021, Available at https://www.ecb.europa.eu/pub/financial-stability/fsr/special/html/ecb.fsrart202105_02~d05518fc6b.en.html

57 Jonathan Schifman, How New York City Found Clean Water, Smithsonian, November 25, 2019, Available at https://www.smithsonianmag.com/history/how-new-york-city-found-clean-water-180973571/

58 Herbert Asbury, The Flour Riot of 1837, The New Yorkers, November 6, 1931 https://www.newyorker.com/magazine/1931/11/14/the-flour-riot-of-1837

59 Paul Krugman, New York Times, OPINION, When Do We Need New Economic Theories? February 8, 2022, Available at https://www.nytimes.com/2022/02/08/opinion/economic-theory-monetary-policy.html

60 UNEP Finance Initiative, History of the Statement, Available at https://www.unepfi.org/about/unep-fi-statement/history-of-the-statement/

61 Paul Clements Hunt worked as the Senior Energy and Environmental Policy Executive (1998-2000) with the Paris-based International Chamber of Commerce (ICC).

62 UNEP Finance Initiative, Values to Value, Available at https://www.unepfi.org/fileadmin/documents/values_to_value_exec_summary_2004.pdf

63 UNEP Finance Initiative, A legal framework for the integration of environmental, social and governance issues into institutional investment, produced for the Asset Management Working Group of the UNEP Finance Initiative, October 2005.

64 UN Habitat & World Bank Group, Multi-Partner Implementation Facility for Sustainable Urban Development – A global programme to achieve sustainable human settlements, Available at https://mirror.unhabitat.org/downloads/docs/13344_1_596141.pdf

65 Derived from 'nine building blocks' outlined in 'Platforms for Partnership' by the Partnering Initiative 2014.

66 THE CODE OF HAMMURABI, based on 1915 translation by L. W. King, Available at http://www.general-intelligence.com/library/hr.pdf

67 Robert Tressell, Project Gutenberg's The Ragged Trousered Philanthropists, Chapter 3: The Financiers provides a vivid illustration of the financial trap of poverty, Available at http://www.gutenberg.org/files/3608/3608-h/3608-h.htm#chap03

68 Scott Corfe & Nigel Keohane, Measuring the Poverty Premium, Social Market Foundation, 2018, Available at https://www.smf.co.uk/wp-content/uploads/2018/03/Measuring-the-Poverty-Premium.pdf

69 Ibid.

70 Ipswich Building Society, A history of building societies – from 1775 to present, 17 Sep 2019 https://www.suffolkbuildingsociety.co.uk/blog/a-history-of-building-societies-from-1775-to-present/

71 UNHCR, Global Report 2019, Available at https://www.unhcr.org/globalreport2019/

72 Dr Mary Tomsic, Learning from the past: Working with WWII refugees, University of Melbourne, https://pursuit.unimelb.edu.au/articles/learning-from-the-past-working-with-wwii-refugees

73 UNHCR, Convention and Protocol relating to the status of refugees, Available at https://www.unhcr.org/en-au/3b66c2aa10

74 UNHCR, Global Compact on Refugees, Available at https://www.unhcr.org/en-au/the-global-compact-on-refugees.html

75 UNHCR Global Compact on Refugees, Pledges, Available at https://globalcompactrefugees.org/article/what-are-pledges

76 See https://globalcompactrefugees.org/channel/pledges-contributions

77 Municipal Forum 2019 Summary Report, UNDP Turkey, January 8, 2020, Available at https://www.tr.undp.org/content/turkey/en/home/library/syria_programme/Municipal-Forum-2019-Event-Summary-Report.html

78 Discussions by Paul Clements Hunt and Gordon Noble with NGOs at the International Forum on Local Solutions to Migration and Displacement held in Gaziantep, Turkey, November 26, 2019, and November 27, 2019.

79 World's negative yield debt pile at 18 trillion for first time, Bloomberg, December 11, 2020, Available at https://www.bloomberg.com/news/articles/2020-12-11/world-s-negative-yield-debt-pile-at-18-trillion-for-first-time

80 Alex Horowitz, A Wealth of Evidence Backs High-Cost Loan Reform, Pew Trust, February 11, 2020, Available at https://www.pewtrusts.org/en/about/news-room/opinion/2020/02/11/a-wealth-of-evidence-backs-high-cost-loan-reform

81 Cortes, Kalena E., Are Refugees Different from Economic Immigrants? Some Empirical Evidence on the Heterogeneity of Immigrant Groups

in the United States (March 2004). Available at SSRN: https://ssrn.com/abstract=524605

82 Bruce Chapman, Timothy Higgins and Joseph Stiglitz (eds) Income Contingent Loans, Theory, Practice and Prospects, International Economic Association, Palgrave macmillan, 2014

83 Friedman, M. (1955) 'The Role of Government in Education', in R. A. Solo (ed.), Economics and the Public Interest (New Brunswick: Rutgers University Press), pp. 123–44 https://la.utexas.edu/users/hcleaver/330T/350kPEEFriedmanRoleOfGovttable.pdf

84 Bruce Chapman, Timothy Higgins and Joseph Stiglitz (eds) Income Contingent Loans, Theory, Practice and Prospects, International Economic Association, Palgrave macmillan, 2014

85 Ibid

86 Bruce Chapman, Income Contingent Loans Background, Chapter 1, in Bruce Chapman, Timothy Higgins and Joseph Stiglitz (eds) Income Contingent Loans, Theory, Practice and Prospects, International Economic Association, Palgrave macmillan, 2014, quoting Bruce Chapman

87 The legal battle to hold the EU to account for Libya migrant abuses, The New Humanitarian, August 10, 2020, Available at https://www.thenewhumanitarian.org/analysis/2020/08/10/Libya-migrant-abuses-EU-legal-battle

88 Linda Botterill, Professor in Australian Politics, University of Canberra, Give people and businesses money now they can pay back later (if and when they can), March 29, 2020, Available at https://theconversation.com/give-people-and-businesses-money-now-they-can-pay-back-later-if-and-when-they-can-134998

89 Commonwealth of Australia, Parliament of Australia 2020, '2019–20 Australian bushfires—frequently asked questions: a quick guide', viewed 27 October 2020, https://www.aph.gov.au/About_Parliament/

Parliamentary_Departments/Parliamentary_Library/pubs/rp/rp1920/Quick_Guides/AustralianBushfires

90 Bank for International Settlements, Basel III: international regulatory framework for banks, Available at https://www.bis.org/bcbs/basel3.htm?m=3%7C14%7C572

91 Australian Prudential Regulation Authority, Capital treatment of investments in the Australian Business Growth Fund, Monday, December 9, 2019, Available at https://www.apra.gov.au/capital-treatment-of-investments-australian-business-growth-fund

92 COVID-19 Increases Urgency for Banks to Transform Payment Systems as Digital Payments Soar, Finds Research from Accenture, Accenture – Newsroom, November 24, 2020, Available at https://newsroom.accenture.com/news/covid-19-increases-urgency-for-banks-to-transform-payment-systems-as-digital-payments-soar-finds-research-from-accenture.htm

93 Immigration and Emigration, BBC, Available at http://www.bbc.co.uk/legacies/immig_emig/england/london/article_1.shtml

94 The Huguenots of Spitalfields, Spitalfields Life, April 14, 2013, Available at https://spitalfieldslife.com/2013/04/14/the-huguenots-of-spitalfields/

95 Paul Clements Hunt and Gordon Noble, Developing a pathway for universal infrastructure coverage, February 28, 2021. This chapter was first published as an essay for the International Institute for Sustainable Development: https://www.iisd.org/publications/developing-pathway-universal-infrastructure-coverage

96 Conceived by The Blended Capital Group at the Infrastructure Investment Frontiers Conference that took place in London on June 6, 2019

97 ECA launches a vehicle for debt management and fiscal sustainability, United Nations Economic Commission for Africa, March 23, 2021, Available at https://www.uneca.org/stories/

eca-launches-lsf,-a-vehicle-for-debt-management-and-fiscal-sustainability

98 UNESCO, The Underground Water Structures in Gaziantep; Livas' and Kastels, Available at https://whc.unesco.org/fr/listesindicatives/6345/

99 UNESCO, The Persian Qanat, Available at https://whc.unesco.org/en/list/1506/

100 UN General Assembly, Resolution adopted by the General Assembly on September 25, 2015, 70/1. Transforming our world: the 2030 Agenda for Sustainable Development http://www.un.org/ga/search/view_doc.asp?symbol=A/RES/70/1&Lang=E

101 Palgrave Studies in Sustainable Business In Association Future Earth, Thomas Walker et al. (Eds), Sustainable Real Estate, Chapter 15 Sustainable Investing in Community Sporting Facilities, 2019

102 Mike Ozanian, World's Most Valuable Sports Teams 2021, Forbes, May 7, 2021, Available at https://www.forbes.com/sites/mikeozanian/2021/05/07/worlds-most-valuable-sports-teams-2021/?sh=-ce728893e9e4

103 Principles for Responsible Investment, Sub-Sovereign Debt, Available at https://www.unpri.org/investment-tools/fixed-income/sub-sovereign-debt

104 Jeremy Gorelick, Lecturer in Emerging Markets Finance, Johns Hopkins University, The real reason why cities in sub-Saharan Africa aren't issuing municipal bonds, February 15, 2018, Available at https://theconversation.com/the-real-reason-why-cities-in-sub-saharan-africa-arent-issuing-municipal-bonds-91688

105 Ibid

106 Ibid

107 US Savings Bond Division, Department of the Treasury, A History of the United States Savings Bond Program, January 1991, Available at https://www.treasurydirect.gov/indiv/research/history/history_sb.pdf

108 Palgrave Studies in Sustainable Business In Association Future Earth, Thomas Walker et al. (Eds), Sustainable Real Estate, Chapter 15: Sustainable Investing in Community Sporting Facilities, 2019

109 UNI Global Union, Including You In A New World Of Work: Background Paper, December 2014.

110 International Monetary Fund, Research Department, Inequality and Labour Market Institutions, Prepared by Florence Jaumotte and Carolina Osorio Buitron, Authorized for distribution by Olivier Blanchard, July 2015

111 Ibid

112 Global Wage Report 2020–21: Wages and minimum wages in the time of COVID-19 International Labor Office – Geneva: ILO, 2020

113 Quoted from The Modern Corporation and the Public Interest, A Speech by John C. Bogle, Founder of the Vanguard Group Before The Public Company Accounting Oversight Board 2017 International Institute, Washington, DC, December 7, 2017

114 David Weil, The Fissured Workplace, Harvard University Press (Kindle Edition), 2014

115 See Humanity United and Verite, Available at https://humanityunited.org/ and https://www.verite.org/

116 Humanity United — Available at https://humanityunited.org/child-labor-can-and-must-be-eradicated/

117 "Sexual Harassment Is Becoming a Serious Investment Risk", Barron's, November 4, 2017

118 Holbeche, Linda; Matthews, Geoffrey. Engaged: Unleashing Your Organization's Potential Through Employee Engagement (p. 6). Wiley. Kindle Edition.

119 Holbeche, Linda; Matthews, Geoffrey. Engaged: Unleashing Your Organization's Potential Through Employee Engagement, Wiley (Kindle Edition), p. 21.

120 Aaron Bernstein and Larry Beeferman, The Materiality of Human Capital to Corporate Financial Performance, April 2015, p. 2

121 Ibid

122 See Human Capital Management Coalition, Available at https://www.hcmcoalition.org/about

123 See Share Action, Workforce Disclosure Initiative, Available at https://shareaction.org/investor-initiatives/workforce-disclosure-initiative

124 Dasgupta, P. (2021), The Economics of Biodiversity: The Dasgupta Review. (London: HM Treasury)

125 IPBES (2019), Global assessment report of the Intergovernmental Science-Policy Platform on Biodiversity and Ecosystem Services, Brondízio, E. S., Settele, J., Díaz, S., Ngo, H. T. (eds). IPBES secretariat, Bonn, Germany (1144 pages, ISBN: 978-3-947851-20-1)

126 Ibid

127 IPCC, 2021: Summary for Policymakers. In: Climate Change 2021: The Physical Science Basis. Contribution of Working Group I to the Sixth Assessment Report of the Intergovernmental Panel on Climate Change [Masson-Delmotte, V., P. Zhai, A. Pirani, S. L. Connors, C. Péan, S. Berger, N. Caud, Y. Chen, L. Goldfarb, M. I. Gomis, M. Huang, K. Leitzell, E. Lonnoy, J.B.R. Matthews, T. K. Maycock, T. Waterfield, O. Yelekçi, R. Yu and B. Zhou (eds.), Cambridge University Press, In Press.

128 Premier of Victoria, Protecting Our Iconic Platypus, January 10, 2021, Available at https://www.premier.vic.gov.au/protecting-our-iconic-platypus

129 Nomination No. 884 Taxon 5136, Flora and Fauna Guarantee – Scientific Advisory Committee Preliminary Recommendation on a Nomination for Listing, Ornithorhynchus anatinus Shaw 1799 – Platypus, Available at https://www.environment.vic.gov.au/__data/assets/pdf_file/0030/484086/01-Platypus-PRR-FinalSign-1.pdf

130 Australian Government, Bureau of Meteorology, State of the Climate 2020, Available at http://www.bom.gov.au/state-of-the-climate/australias-changing-climate.shtml

131 Ibid

132 Frances Mao, How one heatwave killed 'a third' of a bat species in Australia, BBC, January 15, 2019, Available at https://www.bbc.com/news/world-australia-46859000

133 First Nations Australians have lived in Australia for over 60,000 years, AIATSIS, Available at https://aiatsis.gov.au/explore/australias-first-peoples

134 National Gallery Victoria (NGV), https://www.ngv.vic.gov.au/napoleon-and-the-platypus/

135 Centre for Biological Diversity, Halting the Extinction Crisis, Available at https://www.biologicaldiversity.org/programs/biodiversity/elements_of_biodiversity/extinction_crisis/

136 Dasgupta, P. (2021), The Economics of Biodiversity: The Dasgupta Review. (London: HM Treasury)

137 Ibid

138 Victorian Government, Department Land, Environment, Water and Planning, Available at https://www.water.vic.gov.au/water-grid-and-markets/desalination/desalination-background/desalination-history

139 Australian Sustainable Finance Initiative, Australian Sustainable Finance Roadmap, 2020

140 Fish deaths in the Lower Darling, Australian Government, Murray Darling Basin Authority, Available at https://www.mdba.gov.au/issues-facing-basin/fish-deaths/fish-deaths-lower-darling

141 International Capital Markets Association, Sustainability Bond Guidelines, Available at https://www.icmagroup.org/sustainable-finance/the-principles-guidelines-and-handbooks/sustainability-bond-guidelines-sbg/

142 See Report of the Third International Conference on Financing for Development Addis Ababa, 13-16 July 2015, A/CONF.227/20, Available at https://www.undocs.org/A/CONF.227/20

143 Organisation for Economic Co-operation and Development (OECD), Development Co-operation Directorate, Development Assistance Committee, Blended Finance Principles Guidance, DCD/DAC(2020)42/FINAL, September 29, 2020

144 'Daylighting' of Dandenong Creek complete, Living Links, January 13, 2019, Available at https://livinglinks.com.au/daylighting-of-dandenong-creek-complete/

145 Smart water tank to improve platypus, Melbourne Water, Tuesday, August 3, 2021, Available at https://www.melbournewater.com.au/water-data-and-education/news/smart-water-tank-improve-platypus-breeding-odds

146 The Code of Hammurabi, based on 1915 translation by L. W. King, Available at http://www.general-intelligence.com/library/hr.pdf